100

THINGS TO DO IN
DELAWARE
BEFORE YOU
DIE

100

THINGS TO DO IN
DELAWARE
BEFORE YOU
DIE

RACHEL KIPP &
DAN SHORTRIDGE

REEDY PRESS

Reedy Press
PO Box 5131
St. Louis, MO 63139, USA
www.reedypress.com

Library of Congress Control Number: 2020938235

ISBN: 9781681062679

Design by Jill Halpin

Printed in the United States of America
20 21 22 23 24 5 4 3 2 1

DEDICATION

To the kids, who are awesome.

. . . .

CONTENTS

Music and Entertainment

• •

Sports and Recreation

• •

Culture and History

● ●

Shopping and Fashion

• •

PREFACE

One of us grew up in Delaware, and the other came to it for work. Both of us have fallen in love in different ways with the First State and what it offers: close-knit communities, stunning sunsets, well-stocked bookstores, soothing hiking trails, and fantastic food. It's also a great place for children to grow up and explore, which is why we chose to raise our family here and fell in love with the state all over again through the eyes of a teenager and two toddlers.

We hope that this is as much a love letter to Delaware as it is a practical guide to its places, people, and attractions. We had to make some very tough choices in what to include, but ultimately our experiences—from playing skeeball in Rehoboth to walking through the gardens at Hagley—convinced us that these activities and sites represented the best of our home state. We hope that you agree and enjoy the varied experiences that make up Delaware life as much as we do.

Please keep the conversation going and learn about even more events and attractions by following 100 Things to Do in Delaware on Facebook, Instagram, and Twitter at @100thingsinDE or at 100thingsinde.com.

—Rachel and Dan

ACKNOWLEDGMENTS

This book would not have happened if not for the love and support of our family and friends. Special thanks go to Rebecca and Steve Norton, Wendy and Michael Kipp, C. J. and Denise Shortridge, Tom Shortridge, Anna Bowers, and Becky Kipp.

Thanks also to the staff of Delaware Tourism, the Greater Wilmington Convention and Visitors Bureau, Kent County Tourism, Southern Delaware Tourism, the *Kalmar Nyckel*, Winterthur, Hagley Museum and Library, Delaware State Parks, and the Delaware Division of Historic and Cultural Affairs.

An extra-special debt of gratitude is owed to our children Dassi, Mateo, and Liam, who tolerated late hours and being dragged around to odd places in search of facts and photographs. We adore you, and you make us proud every day.

FOOD AND DRINK

GET A FARM-FRESH
TASTE OF DELAWARE ICE CREAM

Agriculture is one of Delaware's biggest sectors, and several entrepreneurial farm families have branched out from simply selling milk to creating and marketing their own ice cream confections. These creameries are active farms as well as ice cream shops, serving up agricultural education along with a scoop. In northern Delaware, the Mitchell family has owned their farm since 1796 and churns out ice cream from its herd of Jersey cows. The University of Delaware's agricultural college runs a campus creamery with ice cream shops in Newark and downtown Wilmington. In Sussex County, the prominent names are Hopkins Farm Creamery, where you can go right up and talk to the cows face-to-face, and Vanderwende Farm Creamery, which has a popular ice cream truck at many festivals and events. The Evans family's Frozen Farmer enterprise, while not a dairy, offers ice cream, sorbets, and "nice cream," a blend of ice cream and sorbet. (You may have seen owner Katey Evans on *Shark Tank*!)

Woodside Farm Creamery
1310 Little Baltimore Rd.
Hockessin, DE 19707
(302) 239-9847
woodsidefarmcreamery.com

UDairy Creamery
531 South College Ave.
Newark, DE 19716
(302) 831-2486
ag.udel.edu/creamery

The Frozen Farmer
9843 Seashore Hwy.
Bridgeville, DE 19933
(302) 337-8130
thefrozenfarmer.com

Hopkins Farm Creamery
Routes 9/404 and Dairy Farm Rd.
Lewes, DE 19958
(302) 645-7163
hopkinsfarmcreamery.com

Vanderwende Farm Creamery
4003 Seashore Hwy.
Bridgeville, DE 19933
(302) 349-5110
vanderwendefarmcreamery.com

TRY SCRAPPLE, A FOOD WITH "EVERYTHING BUT THE SQUEAL"

A list of Delaware delicacies isn't complete without scrapple, a mashup of pork products, cornmeal, flour, and spices that's fried into thin crispy slices. Uncooked, the loaves are grey, mushy, and unappetizing, but once cooked properly with a brown crust, the tastes explode in your mouth with a savory oomph.

Scrapple has been known to trigger countless debates among friends and family. Popular brands include RAPA, Hughes, and Kirby & Holloway, and each has its adherents. But the real controversy surrounds toppings. Do you have your scrapple plain? Served with ketchup? Drizzled with syrup? Or on a sandwich with a slice of cheese?

Join locals in an annual celebration of the treat at the Apple-Scrapple Festival held every October in Bridgeville. (Why apples and scrapple? The town is home to a RAPA scrapple plant and the T. S. Smith & Sons orchards.)

TIP

Many local restaurants serve scrapple as a side at breakfast, or you can pick some up at a butcher shop or grocery store and fry it up on your own. You can also grab a slice on a sandwich each year from the Kirby & Holloway booth at the Delaware State Fair.

FILL YOUR BELLY
AND SATISFY YOUR TASTE BUDS
AT TWO STONES PUB

For a classic gastropub experience, you can't go wrong with Two Stones Pub. Founded with a craft beer focus, its menu also features great grub, and its popularity has just grown, with four locations in Delaware and two across the border in Pennsylvania. If you're a beer fan, you can take your pick from a dynamic revolving selection of craft brews. And if you're a foodie, you absolutely must try the dirty kettle chips—potato chips loaded with cheddar fondue, applewood-smoked bacon, scallions, and gorgonzola, with optional pork or ground chorizo. Its "fry piles" include truffled, hot and spicy, and disco varieties (don't ask; just eat).

Locations in Middletown, Hockessin, Wilmington,
and Newark as well as Kennett Square and Jennersville, PA
twostonespub.com

DID YOU KNOW?

Two Stones' owners have opened three of their locations in vacant strip mall storefronts, investing to help communities revitalize.

FEEL LIKE A KID AGAIN
AT BING'S BAKERY

Bing's is Delaware's longest-running bakery. The family-owned shop originally opened in 1948, and its building at one end of Newark's Main Street is a local landmark. Inside, there's something to satisfy most any sweet tooth and everything you would expect to see at an old-fashioned bakery: a mix-and-match selection of Italian cookies, cheese- and fruit-filled pastries, brownies, sticky buns, and more. Bing's does custom cakes for special occasions, but also has a selection of premade cakes, cheesecakes, pies, and tortes available for walk-in customers. The bakery might also be familiar to fans of "Cake Boss" Buddy Valastro: he visited in 2014 and gave Bing's a modern makeover as part of his TLC show *Buddy's Bakery Rescue*.

253 E. Main St.
Newark, DE 19711
(302) 737-5310
bings@bingsbakery.com
bingsbakery.com

ENJOY
THE QUINTESSENTIAL BEACH TREAT AT DOLLE'S CANDYLAND

Some people will tell you that saltwater taffy, ice cream, or pizza is the top beach treat. Don't let them fool you. In Delaware, that honor goes to Dolle's caramel corn. Available by the bag or bucketful, it's soft and crunchy at the same time, combining sweet and savory tastes in a single bite. The only place to get it is at the beach. The candies are made without preservatives, and the family-owned business doesn't ship its goods elsewhere.

Dolle's is a Rehoboth Beach icon, occupying prime real estate at the corner of Rehoboth Avenue and the boardwalk since 1927. It has survived the Great Depression, World War II, and the Storm of '62, which utterly destroyed the building. Its rooftop script sign, erected after the storm, dominates the skyline and shows up in many vacation snapshots. Dolle's also sells taffy, fudge, and other sweets, and still uses a taffy machine today that was recovered from the sand after the storm.

1 Rehoboth Ave.
Rehoboth Beach, DE 19971
(302) 227-0757
dolles-ibachs.com

TIP

If you want one bag, order two. You won't regret it. Also: hold on to your popcorn around the seagulls that populate the boardwalk!

PICK UP YOUR FAVORITE
ITALIAN TREAT AND SOME TOMATO PIE FOR LATER AT SERPE'S

Serpe's has been a Delaware tradition since 1952, serving Italian sweets, tomato pie, and its famous sandwich rolls, which can also be found at restaurants across the area. (The roll holding together your Capriotti's sub came from here.) The bakery suffered a devastating fire in 2015, but was able to rebuild and held a grand reopening a year later. Crowds line up to get their fill on weekends and holidays. On Christmas Eve alone, Serpe's often fills 1,000 orders. Come early if you want to try the famous tomato pie. It goes fast. But even if you miss out, there will be plenty of breads, rolls, cupcakes, and pastries to sample. Serpe's also does custom orders and has a selection of pasta and other grab-and-go Italian goods for sale.

1411 Kirkwood Hwy.
Elsmere, DE 19805
(302) 994-1868
serpesbakery.com

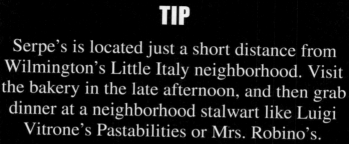

TIP

Serpe's is located just a short distance from Wilmington's Little Italy neighborhood. Visit the bakery in the late afternoon, and then grab dinner at a neighborhood stalwart like Luigi Vitrone's Pastabilities or Mrs. Robino's.

WANDER FOOD HALLS OLD AND NEW
AT DECO WILMINGTON

Food halls have become a popular national trend for showcasing locally grown restaurant talent in a bustling, open-concept atmosphere. Wilmington is home to both a longtime stalwart and a new upstart: the Riverfront Market, which has operated out of a historic warehouse along the Christina River for 20 years, and DECO Wilmington, which opened in 2019 in the historic art deco DuPont Building. DECO's eight vendors include purveyors of pizza, sushi, chicken, and waffles. The Riverfront Market boasts Thai, tacos, and a produce vendor. Both have shared spaces for patrons, many of whom wander over from nearby office buildings to sit and dine.

DECO Wilmington
111 W. 10th St.
Wilmington, DE 19801
info@decowilmington.com
decowilmington.com

The Riverfront Market
3 S. Orange St.
Wilmington, DE 19801
(302) 425-4890

NOSH ON THE BEST BAGELS IN THE STATE,
JUST MINUTES FROM THE BEACH AT SURF BAGEL

Surf Bagel is just what it sounds like—a bagelry at the beach, founded by two brothers who love to surf. The atmosphere is tubular, with surfing decor and televisions showing competitions, but the thick, chewy bagels are just to die for. You can "wax up" your bagel with toppings, but know that the friendly staff is not stingy with the cream cheese. Their "light" is the average person's "really heavy." Get your bagel turned into almost any kind of sandwich or pick up a giant real-fruit smoothie that will tide you over until your next meal. Also served are wraps, hoagies, and soups. The breakfast-and-lunch establishments—one outside Lewes, one near Rehoboth—are also known for their bagel chips. And the menu is kid friendly with PB&J, pizza bagels, and other offerings.

Surf Bagel Lewes
17382 Coastal Hwy.
Lewes, DE 19958
(302) 644-1822

Surf Bagel Rehoboth
18675 Coastal Hwy.
Rehoboth Beach, DE 19971
(302) 644-4822

surfbagel.com

ENJOY FISH & CHIPS
SURROUNDED BY BRITISH ATMOSPHERE AT GO FISH! AND GO BRIT!

If fish and chips is your idea of a treat, there's no better option than sister restaurants go fish! and go brit! at the Delaware beaches. Owned and operated by native Londoner Alyson Blyth, the two serve some of the best comfort food in Delaware, including fish sandwiches and tacos, tandoori chicken, and the best shepherd's pie you'll have on this side of the pond. Go fish, a block from the beach in Rehoboth, has a cozy, intimate atmosphere festooned with Union Jacks and "mind the gap" signs. Go brit, a larger eatery on Route 1 between Lewes and Rehoboth, offers largely the same fare, ordered at a counter. Both establishments feature their signature desserts, including to-die-for sticky toffee pudding. You won't regret tucking in for a meal at either!

go fish!
24 Rehoboth Ave.
Rehoboth Beach, DE 19971
(302) 226-1044
gofishrehoboth.com

go brit!
18388 Coastal Hwy.
Lewes, DE 19958
(302) 644-2250
gobrit.com

DON'T MISS
THE MILK SHAKES OR THE BURGERS AT THE CHARCOAL PIT

It's known as the "Pit" to its most die-hard customers, but don't let the name turn you off. The Charcoal Pit has been a northern Delaware institution for more than 60 years, supplying legions of families—and one burger-loving vice president—with fuel. The classic casual burger-joint atmosphere doesn't mean that's all it serves; the Pit has a full menu of sandwiches, salads, and entrees as well. The thick hand-dipped shakes are a must with any meal, and the sundaes bear the names of local schools, like the "Highlander" for McKean High School, with vanilla ice cream, hot fudge, bananas, walnuts, and whipped cream. (All get at least one cherry on top.)

North Wilmington (original location)
2600 Concord Pike
Wilmington, DE 19803
(302) 478-2165
Prices Corner
Kirkwood Hwy. and Greenbank Rd.
(302) 998-8853

charcoalpit.net

HAVE SOME SASS WITH YOUR BREAKFAST
AT LUCKY'S

You'll smile when you step into Lucky's Coffee Shop, whether it's due to the great smells wafting from the kitchen, the irreverent T-shirts worn by the staff, or the spinning egg chair beloved by the kids. While it's called a coffee shop, Lucky's is so much more than that, serving a full menu for breakfast, lunch, and dinner. Even the menu is sassy: the description of a BLT says "really? you're looking for a description of this?!!" The sandwiches are great (they do a stellar veggie burger), but breakfast is the star here. You can't go wrong with eggs, sausage, and a giant serving of either home fries or hash. And don't miss out on the super-thick-sliced soft brioche French toast!

4003 Concord Pike
Wilmington, DE 19803
(302) 477-0240
luckyscoffeeshop.com

MEET YOUR LOCAL FARMERS
AT COMMUNITY FARMERS MARKETS

Bright red strawberries; heavy, full watermelons; and ripe, juicy peaches— why not buy them directly from the farmers who grew them? Delaware's farmers market program offers a chance to stock up on produce and other farm products and have a chat with the farmer down the road at the same time. The open-air markets—numbering around 20 each year—are run by local governments, chambers of commerce, and nonprofits.

Stroll by tables piled high with fresh fruits and veggies, pick up breads, eggs, and milk, and spy out locally produced jams and jellies. If you have questions about your lima beans, pumpkins, or asparagus, farmers are happy to offer cooking and storage suggestions, and you walk away feeling good about supporting local family farmers. Many markets also accept SNAP benefits, coupons for WIC participants, and vouchers for senior citizens to help stretch those dollars.

Buy Local Delaware Guide
Delaware Department of Agriculture
(302) 698-4500
de.gov/buylocal

EAT SAUSAGE
MADE BY "THE KING"
AT MAIALE DELI & SALUMERIA

Chef Billy Rawstrom calls himself the "Sausage King of Delaware," and you'll be a loyal subject after just one visit to his Wilmington shop. Maiale (the Italian word for "pig") features an extensive grab-and-go menu of sausage—from standards, such as sweet and spicy Italian, kielbasa, andouille, and chorizo, to more adventurous blends; turkey sausage with dried cranberries, wild boar sausage with apples, caramelized onions and goat cheese, and duck sausage with cherries and goat cheese. You'll also find several different types of salami and cured meat for sale.

If you've got time, sit down and have breakfast or lunch at the shop. The menu includes such signature sandwiches as the award-winning "Mexicano burger," with ground chuck, roasted poblano peppers, cilantro, and cumin on a kaiser roll topped with pickled onion, Chihuahua cheese, and chipotle, and "the Castro," made of house-cured ham, roast pork, Swiss cheese, pickles, and Dijonnaise sauce on pressed French bread, which was featured on a segment about Maiale on Food Network's *Diners, Drive-ins and Dives*. Rawstrom also hosts tasting dinners at Maiale and classes, including a "snout to tail" course where a chef breaks down a 240-pound pig and discusses the best ways to use different cuts.

3301 Lancaster Pike
Wilmington, DE 19805
(302) 691-5269
thesausagekingofdelaware.com

TIP

In addition to the shop just outside downtown Wilmington, Maiale sets up at local farmers markets during the summer and contributes menu items to the Constitution Yards beer garden on the Wilmington riverfront.

RELAX WITH A DINNER
OF CLASSIC COMFORT SEAFOOD
AT MATT'S FISH CAMP

The late Delaware chef Matt Haley's legacy of great food and customer service is epitomized by the eatery that bears his name, Matt's Fish Camp. The cheerful and informal atmosphere belies the top-notch comfort food offerings, such as crab cakes, short-rib grilled cheese sandwiches, fried chicken, and biscuits. The chicken pot pie is a classic, hearty meal with a tender biscuit for a lid. But don't even think about eating here without a double order—at least—of the melt-in-your-mouth Parker House rolls, baked by Old World Breads. They're the perfect complement to the clam chowder, shrimp, and lobster rolls. And for families, there are plenty of kid-friendly, grown-up-style offerings, such as fish and chips, grilled salmon, and fried shrimp that both parents and kids alike will appreciate.

Matt's Fish Camp Bethany
28635 Coastal Hwy.
Bethany Beach, DE 19930
(302) 539-2267
mattsfishcampbethany.com

Matt's Fish Camp Lewes
33401 Tenley Court
Lewes, DE 19958
(302) 644-2267
mattsfishcamplewes.com

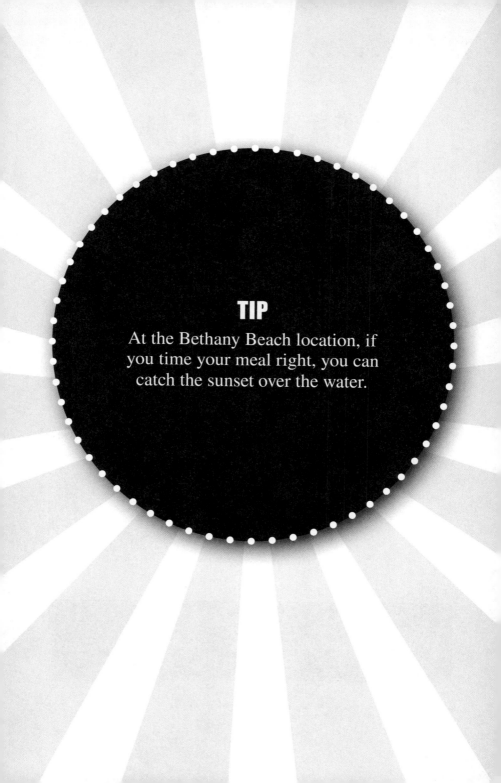

TIP

At the Bethany Beach location, if you time your meal right, you can catch the sunset over the water.

PICK YOUR OWN
FRUITS AND VEGGIES
RIGHT OFF THE VINE

Unless you're a farmer yourself, there's no way of getting closer to the land and the food you eat than by picking it directly from the tree, bush, or vine. U-pick farms offer a great day of family fun and can create enduring childhood memories plus lots of laughter and great photos of the see kids wandering out of the strawberry rows covered in telltale red juices. (You usually pay by the basket or pound on the honor system, so don't do too much snacking in the fields!) Some farms offer a hayride to the picking area for even more shared fun. The state's diverse family-run farms offer opportunities throughout the season to gather your own Delaware-grown peaches, nectarines, apples, strawberries, blueberries, pumpkins, sunflowers, and much more.

Buy Local Delaware Guide
Delaware Department of Agriculture
(302) 698-4500
de.gov/buylocal

TIP
Go during the early morning or late afternoon to deflect the worst of the summer heat. Plus wear a hat and sunscreen!

EAT THE LUNCH
THAT A VICE PRESIDENT MADE
FAMOUS AT CAPRIOTTI'S

Then-Vice President Joe Biden made headlines when he visited the first Washington, DC, outpost of this family-owned sandwich shop. Though Capriotti's now has locations in more than a dozen states, it all started with one shop that opened in 1976 in Wilmington's Little Italy neighborhood. Siblings Lois and Alan Margolet opened this shop named after their grandfather Capriotti in the boarded-up building beneath their apartment.

The menu includes sandwiches and subs for any kind of palate, but Capriotti's is most famous for The Bobbie: homemade turkey, cranberry sauce, stuffing, and mayo on a sub roll that's the perfect balance between crusty and soft. The sandwich is also one of Biden's favorites. When he visited the DC location on opening day, he reportedly ordered one with hot peppers on the side. It's a lot of tasty carbs packed into one sandwich, and Capriotti's veterans recommend splitting one—and planning a brisk walk around the block afterward.

Locations throughout the state
capriottis.com

TIP
The chain's corporate offices have since relocated to Las Vegas, but the original Little Italy location is still open at 510 Union Street, Wilmington.

ENHANCE
YOUR FIRST STATE PALATE
WITH DELAWARE-MADE WINES

Delaware isn't widely known for its wines, but it should be. The small state is home to four home-grown vineyards, each with its own focus and specialties. These out-of-the-way, off-the-beaten-path establishments are family-owned labors of love, and that love shines through in their offerings. The oldest, Nassau Valley Vineyards, is just over 30 years old, and two—Harvest Ridge and Salted Vines—have popped up in the last decade. From merlots to chardonnays, there's something for every wine enthusiast. For those looking to hold an event, several wineries have tasting rooms and facilities suitable for a special day!

Harvest Ridge Winery and Rebel Seed Cidery
477 Westville Rd.
Marydel, DE 19964
(302) 343-9437
harvestridgewinery.com

Pizzadili Vineyard and Winery
1683 Peach Basket Rd.
Felton, DE 19943
(302) 284-9463
pizzadiliwinery.com

Nassau Valley Vineyards
32165 Winery Way
Lewes, DE 19968
(302) 645-9463
nassauvalley.com

Salted Vines Vineyard and Winery
32512 Blackwater Rd.
Frankford, DE 19945
(302) 436-1500
saltedvines.com

18

REAP THE REWARDS
OF BEING AN EARLY RISER
AT HELEN'S SAUSAGE HOUSE

Pigs and Elvis dominate the down-home decor at Helen's Sausage House, a Smyrna institution that is equally famous for its menu and its unusual hours. Catering to truckers, the restaurant opens at 4:00 a.m. each day and closes by noon (2:00 p.m. on Mondays). Those who show up later in the morning should expect a packed parking lot and a line inside, but it moves quickly. The menu features standard breakfast and lunch food, such as omelettes and subs, but the real star is Helen's famous sausage sandwich: two jumbo sausage links grilled to perfection on a bun with optional fried green peppers and onions. You can also buy uncooked sausage to bring home.

4866 N. Dupont Hwy.
Smyrna, DE 19977
(302) 653-4200

TIP
Helen's is cash only (there is an ATM on the premises).

26

GRAB A MEAL
ON THE GO
AT OLD WORLD BREADS

Old World Breads offers everything you need for a hearty meal or snack on the go—and plenty to take home and enjoy once your adventure is over. Conveniently located next to the trailhead of a popular local walking and biking path, the bakery offers a full lunch menu, including salads, soups, sandwiches, and flatbread pizzas, most of them homemade with locally sourced ingredients. For breakfast, there are towering egg sandwiches (come early; they sell out fast, especially on summer weekends), quiches, and several different varieties of croissants and pastries. There is also a full menu of breads, including baguettes, three kinds of Italian, orange cardamom, cranberry walnut, multigrain, and more. Note that all bread is made traditionally, without preservatives. If you take a loaf home, eat it within two days or freeze it to eat later.

32191 Nassau Rd.
Lewes, DE 19958
(302) 313-5191
oldworldbreads.com

TIP

Old World is worth stopping by on Mondays for its "Day Old Bake Sale." You can stock up at discount prices until they sell out. Arrive close to the 7:00 a.m. opening time for the biggest variety.

SAMPLE 100 DIFFERENT FLAVORS OF ICE CREAM
AT THE BEACH

A sure sign of warmer weather in Delaware is the annual opening of the Ice Cream Store, a beachside ice cream shop that has become famous for off-the-wall—but delicious—flavors, such as Booger (green cake batter ice cream with green caramel swirl and marshmallow bits), Crack (brown sugar and vanilla ice cream with pasteurized egg yolks, butter, and sea salt), and Better than Sex (cake batter ice cream with Duncan Hines Devil's Food cake mix, African vanilla extract, Heath bars, and fudge). About 100 different flavors are on the menu at any given time, but they switch out weekly, and sampling is encouraged. All of the homemade flavors are made with milk from the cows at Delaware's Woodside Creamery.

6 Rehoboth Ave.
Rehoboth Beach, DE 19971
(302) 227-4609, rehobothbeachicecream.com

TIP

Ice Cream Store owner Chip Hearn also runs an online hot sauce business, Peppers.com, which has a physical location open year-round in Lewes. The two passions have produced several pepper-laced ice cream flavors that require customers to sign a waiver before tasting.

TRY "UNAPOLOGETICALLY VEGAN" FOOD
AT DROP SQUAD KITCHEN

Tucked into an out-of-the-way storefront shared with an ice cream shop on Wilmington's riverfront, Drop Squad Kitchen offers inventive vegan food that even meat lovers will appreciate. Owner Abundance Child began introducing the cuisine at her parents' ice cream shop in 2012. Everything at Drop Squad, which takes its name from a 1994 Spike Lee movie, is made from scratch to order. Settle in at one of the handful of tables inside and order a drink while you wait. A customer favorite is the Rose Quartz—fresh citrus lemonade with a shot of Hi Red (hibiscus, ginger, and lemon juice). The menu's soups, salads, sandwiches, and tacos feature vegan beef, chicken, fish, cheese, sour cream, mayo, and more. Top off any order with a side of kettle-cooked sweet potato chips.

928 Justison St.
Wilmington, DE 19801
(302) 984-2773
dropsquadkitchen.com

TIP
Check the glass case up front for a selection of vegan desserts.

PICK YOUR SIDE
IN THE GREAT PIZZA DEBATE

Delaware is a state of pizza enthusiasts with great loyalty to their particular pies. The dominant local pizza purveyor is Grotto, a homegrown chain with roots in Rehoboth Beach, which has expanded its swirled-sauce style to more than 16 locations in Delaware and three in Maryland. (Some locations feature sports bars and kid-friendly game areas.) Also on Rehoboth Avenue is Nicola Pizza, noted for both its pizzas and famous "Nic-O-Bolis"—sauce, cheeses, and toppings baked in dough. Upstate fans highly recommend Cafe Riviera, located in an unassuming spot in the Concord Mall but boasting fantastic tomato pies, and DiMeo's in downtown Wilmington, where fighting over a spot at lunch for its Neapolitan-style pies is worth it. And for an unforgettable gourmet experience, there's Pizza by Elizabeths, which is as close to fine dining as you can get while eating pizza. Every pie is named after a famous Elizabeth, e.g., the Queen (mushroom duxelles sauce, chicken, parmesan, and chives) and Shue (BBQ chicken, mozzarella, and fontina).

Grotto Pizza
With more than 16 locations in all three counties, one's always close by.
grottopizza.com

Nicola Pizza
8 N. First St. or 71 Rehoboth Ave.
Rehoboth Beach, DE 19971
(302) 227-6211, nicolapizza.com

Cafe Riviera
Located inside the Concord Mall
4737 Concord Pike
Wilmington, DE 19810
(302) 478-8288
caferiviera@comcast.net
www.caferivierade.com

DiMeo's Pizza
831 N. Market St.
Wilmington, DE 19801
(302) 655-1427, dimeospizza.com

Pizza by Elizabeths
3801 Kennet Pike
Greenville, DE 19807
(302) 654-4478
pizzabyelizabeths.com

DINE AT A PLACE
WITH A NUMBER IN THE NAME

Restaurant 55 and 33 West sometimes get mixed up by visitors because of their names, but the truth is they're very different eateries—both offering some of Kent County's finest food. Located on an unassuming road heading out of Dover, Restaurant 55 is a local secret—a gourmet burger joint with the dark, intimate feel of a brewpub. Its meat and vegetables come from local butchers and farms. You've got to try the NFB—Not For Breakfast—a sage burger topped with fried egg, cheese, and bacon. At 33 West, enjoy a local craft beer while digging into upscale American grub. It's a small establishment on a corner of downtown Dover's main drag that often draws hungry locals looking for great food during a business lunch, so arrive as early as you can to get a table! The black bean burger is a special treat, the crisp fries are fantastic, and the fried calamari is a hit with children lucky enough to tag along.

Restaurant 55
2461 S. State St.
Dover, DE 19901
(302) 535-8102
myrestaurant55.com

33 West
33 W. Loockerman St.
Dover, DE 19904
(302) 735-9822
facebook.com/33Westalehouse

EAT WITH A VIEW
OF THE GOVERNOR'S MANSION
AT GOVERNOR'S CAFE

Located across the street from Woodburn, the official residence of Delaware's governor, Governor's Cafe is the perfect spot to enjoy a lazy afternoon. Housed in a historic mansion built in 1857, the cafe features a wide, welcoming front porch and several rooms inside decorated with images of all 71 Delaware governors. There's a full menu for more upscale sit-down dinners and lunches. But you can also walk in, grab a sandwich or cup of coffee, settle in at a table in- or outside, read, catch up on work or email, or play one of the board games the cafe keeps on hand.

144 Kings Hwy.
Dover, DE 19901
(302) 747-7531
governorscafe.de

EAT FOOD MADE FOR EVERY DIET
AT HOME GROWN CAFE

Situated in the middle of Newark's Main Street, Home Grown Cafe prides itself on having something for everyone, whether you're a meat lover, gluten free, vegetarian, or vegan.

The food is made from scratch, and most of the menu items are adaptable based on diet (they're all helpfully marked). Highlights include the Kennett Square mushroom soup and the Green Goddess sandwich with avocado, Muenster cheese, local sprout and shoot salad, tomatoes, arugula, and green goddess dressing on wheat bread.

While you eat, keep your eyes on the walls. They're decorated with the work of local artists, which is available for sale. Home Grown also features local music acts on Wednesday and Saturday evenings, but it's got a more low-key vibe than some of the more traditional college restaurants and bars in town.

126 E. Main St.
Newark, DE 19711
(302) 266-6993, homegrowncafe.com

TIP
Since many of Home Grown Cafe's menu items featuring meat are customizable for herbivores, make sure to specify when ordering if you want it vegan or vegetarian.

FOLLOW IN THE
FOOTSTEPS OF WASHINGTON AND POE AT DEER PARK TAVERN

The site of Newark's Deer Park Tavern has offered respite to weary travelers since the Revolutionary War. Saint Patrick's Inn opened there in 1747, and it is believed that George Washington once spent the night. Perhaps the most fateful day in the inn's history was December 23, 1843, when Edgar Allen Poe, visiting Newark to lecture at the precursor to the University of Delaware, fell in the mud outside and put a curse on the building. The inn, a three-story log cabin, burned to the ground several years later.

The Deer Park Tavern took its place and since 1851 has served as a hotel, barbershop, ballroom, and (rumor has it) a stop on the Underground Railroad. These days the street outside is thankfully paved, and patrons come to the Deer Park for burgers, brunch, and happy hour. For lunch, try the Farmhouse Burger with an Angus beef patty, a fried egg, cheddar, bacon, and mushrooms from nearby Kennett Square, PA. On the weekends, an extensive brunch menu offers eggs just about any way you'd like them. If you stop in on a Sunday, try the Food Truck Tots (named because they're from the menu of the owner's food truck, the Roaming Raven), tater tots covered with pulled pork, melted jack cheese, and two fried eggs.

108 W. Main St.
Newark, DE 19711
(302) 369-9414, deerparktavern.com

HAVE A PLEASANTLY
OFF-CENTERED EXPERIENCE
AT DOGFISH HEAD

Dogfish Head is famous around the world for its creative take on craft beer. Founder Sam Calagione started brewing beer in his kitchen in New York City. When the original Dogfish Head location opened in 1995, it produced 10 gallons a day. Now merged with the Boston Beer Co., the company makes its home in a converted cannery in the inland town of Milton and produces more than 15,000 gallons daily.

The Dogfish Head empire at the Delaware beaches now includes the Milton brewery; the original location in Rehoboth Beach, which is now a brewpub; the restaurant next door, Chesapeake and Maine, which focuses on seafood and spirits; and an inn in Lewes.

A trip to any of these will be fun even for those who don't like beer, and it's friendly for the entire family. The Milton brewery offers several tour and tasting options and offers a peek into how Calagione incorporates local ingredients into his beers. Food is available on the premises, and children are welcome (but Dogfish Head cautions visitors to be prepared for a PG-13 tour).

In addition to a full menu (try the pretzel bites), the Rehoboth brewpub has Dogfish beers on its menu that you won't find anywhere else. Have a fancy dinner at Chesapeake & Maine, where you can sample the raw bar and enjoy the fanciful murals on the walls. The inn boasts a fridge stocked with locally made snacks, a free 32-oz. growler, and Dogfish-branded chicory stout coffee.

Dogfish Head Brewery
6 Cannery Village Center
Milton, DE 19968
(888) 8-DOGFISH, dogfish.com

Dogfish Head Brewings & Eats
320 Rehoboth Ave.
Rehoboth Beach, DE 19971
(302) 226-BREW
dogfish.com/restaurants/brewpub

Chesapeake & Maine
316 Rehoboth Ave.
Rehoboth Beach, DE 19971
(302) 226-3600
dogfish.com/restaurants/chesapeake-maine

The Dogfish Inn
105 Savannah Rd.
Lewes, DE 19958
(302) 644-8292, dogfish.com/inn

DID YOU KNOW?

During the coronavirus outbreak in spring 2020, Dogfish retooled part of its distillery to make hand sanitizer, selling it at market price to the state government, and donating all proceeds to a fund to help restaurant workers.

DINE
IN THE FIRST JEWISH DELI IN DELAWARE AT ROSENFELD'S

Caricatures of famous Jewish people line the walls at the Rehoboth Beach location of Rosenfeld's Deli, a chain which, upon opening in 2013 in Ocean City, Maryland, became the only restaurant of its kind for two hours in any direction.

Rosenfeld's came to the Delaware beaches in 2017 and plans to expand to a location in Wilmington in 2020. Owner Warren Rosenfeld comes from a family of restaurateurs: his grandfather co-owned and ran a bakery in Washington, DC's Eastern Market, and his parents ran a diner there for 15 years. He describes Rosenfeld's as a "Jewish food museum," and lovers of the cuisine will find all of their favorites: pickles, smoked fish platters, latkes, kugels, knishes, towering piles of pastrami or brisket on rye, Dr. Brown's soda, and chocolate egg creams. There's also all-day breakfast and a mini-menu of kosher hot dogs.

You can buy challah, smoked fish, and meats by the pound to take home. And you will want to pick up something from the dessert case, which is filled with giant slices of cheesecake, carrot cake, and more.

18949 Coastal Hwy.
Rehoboth Beach, DE 19971
(302) 645-1700
rosenfeldsjewishdeli.com

1204 Washington St.
Wilmington, DE 19801
(Location will open in 2020)

ENJOY A VIEW
OF THE BEACH AND THE BRIDGE
AT BIG CHILL BEACH CLUB

When Big Chill Beach Club opened atop the bathhouse at Delaware Seashore State Park in 2017, it was the biggest public/private partnership and capital investment in Delaware park history.

The effort created a truly unique dining experience, with 360-degree views of the Atlantic Ocean, the Delaware Bay, and the Indian River Inlet Bridge. Enjoy the outdoor fire pit and sand pit area, or eat in the rooftop umbrella "room" and bar designed to withstand rain and winds up to 100 mph. The seafood-centric menu includes conch fritters and tuna poke appetizers and tacos filled with mahi mahi, grilled shrimp, or cod. There's also a full bar offering cocktails, beer, and wine.

27099 Coastal Hwy.
Bethany Beach, DE 19930
(302) 402-5300
bigchillbeachclub.com

TIP
You can take food from Big Chill onto the beach, but alcohol has to stay on the premises.

MUSIC AND ENTERTAINMENT

CATCH A MOVIE
IN AN OLD-FASHIONED ONE-SCREEN CINEMA AT CLAYTON THEATRE

The Clayton Theatre, located in tiny Dagsboro, just marked its 70th year, having overcome corporate consolidation, demographic changes, and the switch to digital projection. It still shows first-run movies on its single screen—Delaware's only surviving theatre of that type. The movie-watching experience at the Clayton is cozy, with seating available in the main area or the balcony. At night, the marquee lights up in green and pink neon in a retro callback to yesteryear. Tickets remain affordable at this local landmark and historic venue just a short trip from the beaches, and it has plenty of snacks and popcorn to round out your traditional movie night. Worth noting: the Clayton's fans are devoutly loyal, having raised enough money a few years ago to help the theatre cover the cost of converting from 35mm to digital projection.

33246 Main St.
Dagsboro, DE 19939
Box Office: (302) 732-3744
Main: (302) 732-9606
theclaytontheatre.com

LIVE THE SIGHTS, SOUNDS, AND SMELLS
OF THE STATE FAIR

Like many local fairs, the Delaware State Fair has grown from an agricultural expo to a 10-day entertainment extravaganza. Each July, nationally acclaimed musicians and comedians alternate center stage with a down-home demolition derby and horse racing. But farming remains at the fair's core, with animals and 4-H exhibitions still a huge draw for many visitors. Watching young people proudly show off their cows, horses, and goats to nationally renowned judges is a special heartwarming highlight. And for families not involved in agriculture, where else can you pet a pig, ride a spinning contraption, get a henna tattoo, eat fried Twinkies, rub elbows with campaigning politicians, and hold a baby chick all in the span of an hour?

18500 S. DuPont Hwy.
Harrington, DE 19952
(302) 398-3269
delawarestatefair.com

TIP

Save a few bucks on admission by presenting nonperishable goods on Hunger Relief Day or bringing your kids in free on Kids' Day.

TAKE A RELAXING RIDE
ON AN OLD-FASHIONED RAILWAY

Except for taking high-speed rail between major cities, riding the train these days seems quaint and outdated, a relic of bygone times. That's exactly the reason that the Wilmington & Western Railroad exists—to keep up the heritage of train travel. The seats squeak, there's no Wi-Fi, power outlets are nonexistent, and a locomotive with its classic stark profile sits at the head of the line. The railroad runs regular steam- and diesel-powered tourist trains from the spring through December on a 10-mile stretch of track between Greenbank Station and Hockessin. You can ride the train, enjoy the scenic views, stop for a picnic on the banks of Red Clay Creek, and shop at your destination. (There are also shorter routes available for younger passengers who may not have the stamina for a full ride.)

Greenbank Station
2201 Newport Gap Pike
(Route 41 North)
Wilmington, DE 19808

Office & Education Center
1601 Railroad Ave.
Wilmington, DE 19808
(302) 998-1930, wwrr.com

TIP
You can charter the entire train, a single car, or the red caboose for group events. The caboose is perfect for small birthday parties, especially for train-loving youngsters.

DID YOU KNOW?

The railroad was beset with natural disasters from 1999 to 2003, with many track washouts and destroyed bridges because of Hurricane Floyd and Tropical Storm Henri. After the latter, it took four years, until 2007, to fully rebuild and have trains running the complete route again.

CHECK OUT INDEPENDENT
FILMS FROM AROUND THE GLOBE AT WILMINGTON'S ONLY ART HOUSE CINEMA

Tucked among the offices and conference rooms in downtown Wilmington's historic art deco Nemours Building, Theatre N is truly a hidden gem. A project of former Wilmington Mayor James Baker, the one-screen theatre opened in 2002 and features a state-of-the-art digital projection and sound system. You can see movies here that you won't find anywhere else in the state, and some that might even be hard to catch at art house theatres up the road in Philadelphia. Among them are American indie movies but also documentaries and foreign films. Each year around Oscar time, Theatre N shows all of the nominated shorts in the documentary and animation categories. There are also regular opera and ballet screenings and late-night showings of *The Rocky Horror Picture Show* on Saturdays.

1007 N. Orange St., inside the Nemours Building
Wilmington, DE 19801
(302) 571-4075
boxoffice@theatren.com
theatren.com

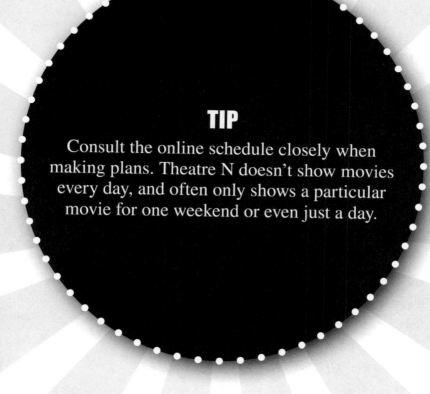

TIP

Consult the online schedule closely when making plans. Theatre N doesn't show movies every day, and often only shows a particular movie for one weekend or even just a day.

RIDE AN
OLD-FASHIONED MERRY-GO-ROUND AT FUNLAND

For classic, wholesome family fun, you can't go wrong with a ride on a merry-go-round, and Delaware's signature carousel is found near Rehoboth Beach's boardwalk. The merry-go-round at Funland, a nearly 60-year-old attraction, can be found pumping out music and spinning children and their parents around, up, and down on wooden horses just steps from the sand and surf. The merry-go-round is one of a handful of rides at the family-owned amusement park that dates back to before its founding in 1962, but the staff keeps it running smoothly, with colors and lights shining as brightly today as they did when the ponies were first painted.

For children who claim to be too old for a merry-go-round (really, no one is *too old*), Funland has a host of other options, including a haunted house, bumper cars, the stomach-turning spinning Gravitron, and old-fashioned games that won't bust anyone's budget. Ride tickets are good for life, so don't worry about buying too many because you can always use them next year!

6 Delaware Ave.
Rehoboth Beach, DE 19971
(302) 227-1921
funlandrehoboth.com

TIP

Opening times are listed on the park's website. Closing times can vary depending on weather and attendance; during the height of the summer, the park usually won't shut down before 11:00 p.m. Funland is open May to September.

EXPERIENCE
THE "MONSTER MILE"
WITH TOP NASCAR DRIVERS
AT DOVER INTERNATIONAL SPEEDWAY

Twice a year, Delaware is host to the best racing in the world, as NASCAR drivers swoop into the First State for two action-packed, speed-driven weekends in May and August. On Friday, Saturday, and Sunday, the Dover International Speedway at Dover Downs Hotel & Casino hosts three consecutive races, including a NASCAR Cup Series race. Racing fans from all over come to see and hear the cars rocket around the track 400 times at a track-record speed of 135 mph. It's called the "Monster Mile," and devoted fans can even pay to drive the oval or go for spins with a racing school instructor.

For non-racing fans, it's a great people-watching exercise too! Dover, the state capital, is flooded with visitors; businesses turn over their parking lots to RVs, and nearby fields fill up with campers and tents days before racing begins. And the casino is happy to host anyone who needs a break and wants to test their luck!

1131 N. Dupont Hwy.
Dover, DE 19901
Tickets: (800) 441-RACE
Main: (302) 883-6500
doverspeedway.com

BE ENTERTAINED
AT MIDDLETOWN'S CENTURY-OLD HUB FOR THE ARTS IN THE EVERETT THEATRE

Opened in 1922 as the local movie house, the Everett Theatre was redeveloped in the 1980s as home to a local nonprofit arts hub, breathing new life into the space. Outside of Delaware, it's best known as the theatre in the 1989 movie *Dead Poets Society*, which was filmed in Middletown. Today, the theatre has one black seat to mark the legacy of the film's star Robin Williams.

Before you think that 1989 was the high-water mark for this community centerpiece, think again. Middletown is one of the fastest-growing towns in the state, and the Everett has filled the need for artistic expressions with live community theatre (showcasing such classics as *West Side Story* and *South Pacific*), movies, classes, art exhibits, and summer camps where children put on performances, such as *The Lion King Jr.*, *Sweeney Todd* (the school edition), and *High School Musical Jr.* There's even a basics camp for younger children between ages 4 and 7 to ensure the next generations are prepared to enjoy the arts.

47 W. Main St.
Middletown, DE 19709
(302) 232-6338
info@everetttheatre.com
everetttheatre.com

TAKE A LESSON
AT DELAWARE'S HOMEGROWN MUSIC SCHOOL

Good music is timeless, and the Music School of Delaware is nearly so, having been a First State institution for nearly 100 years. It really is open to all ages. Young children take beginning piano lessons in study rooms next to septuagenarians practicing violin or voice. Programs include rock, jazz, and folk music; ensembles such as orchestral, choral, and chamber music; and music therapy. The school has more than 90 instructors with flexible schedules, so you can usually find a day and time that work for you. And for music fans who prefer listening to performing, the music school holds more than 100 public performances and workshops throughout the year. There are locations in both Wilmington and Milford, so wherever you live there are classes close by.

Wilmington Branch
4101 Washington St.
Wilmington, DE 19802
(302) 762-1132

Milford Branch
23 N. Walnut St.
Milford, DE 19963
(302) 422-2043

musicschoolofdelaware.org

TAKE
THE CAPE MAY-LEWES FERRY FOR A QUICK TRIP TO JERSEY

If you've seen all you can see in Delaware (even though that's really not possible), have a unique travel experience aboard the Cape May–Lewes Ferry: a trip of just over an hour that will take you from the cozy beach town of Lewes to bustling Cape May, New Jersey. It's a relaxing way to commute—and some people do commute by ferry every day for work—that will have you looking out rather than down at your phone. A ferry trip means enjoying pleasant weather, watching dolphins at play, and admiring the scenery of local lighthouses. There's air conditioning, TV, and Wi-Fi access as well. If you come aboard on foot, catch a seasonal shuttle bus to your destination on either end. The ferry terminals aren't just boring harbors, but host a variety of festivals and events year-round!

43 Cape Henlopen Dr.
Lewes, DE 19958
(800) 643-3779

DID YOU KNOW?

The ferry is actually three vessels that ply the tides back and forth across the 17-mile-wide Delaware Bay.

TO WIN AT SKEEBALL,
IT'S ALL IN THE WRIST

If you've never played skeeball—or even heard of it—then you're missing out. Skeeball (or skee-ball) is a challenging and loud arcade game that dates back to the early 1900s. Players roll a hard ball up an incline and over a bump, with the goal of earning points by depositing the ball in numbered holes. Rumble-rumble-rumble is the constant sound at a skeeball game. It's incredibly addictive, and you often see whole families lined up at the ramps laughing and competing against each other. Several arcades along the Rehoboth Beach Boardwalk offer the game, with prices ranging from a dime to a quarter. At Funland, you can win small stuffed animals and trade them in for larger ones as you keep winning; at Zelky's, you win tickets and can trade them in for all types of prizes.

TIP

If you win tickets but don't want to use them right away, hold onto them; most of the arcades will let you trade them in indefinitely (the same is true of Funland's distinctive green ride tickets).

TAKE IN A SHOW
AT THE RESTORED THEATRE
ON THE RIVERBANKS

Back in the day, every town had a local theatre, and Milton—a small picturesque town on the banks of the Broadkill River—was no exception. Its theatre, right on the main downtown street, fell into disrepair by the 1990s, but a community fundraising and restoration effort brought the building back to its former glory, and work is now underway to rebuild the balcony. It's a cozy, intimate theatre whose original brick walls host everything from school plays to *The Rocky Horror Picture Show* nights. Traveling John Denver tribute artists share the stage with Disney movies and handbell ensembles, and the theatre's supporters run local musical productions and superhero tea events for children, along with a full suite of summer programs.

The Milton Theatre
110 Union St.
Milton, DE 19968
(302) 684-3038, miltontheatre.com

TIP
The theatre serves refreshments and light fare, but you can stop in at local eateries along Union Street and then take a post-dinner stroll along the riverwalk to make it a full night out.

VISIT THE ANIMALS
AT DELAWARE'S LONE ZOO

Delaware's a small state with a small zoo, but one with a lot of animals to learn about! Brandywine Zoo has a red panda, pygmy goats, a capybara, a Florida bobcat, a bald eagle, a green tree python, and Italian honeybees! One of the most striking creatures is an Andean Condor, a type of vulture that looks down on visitors from its high perches. The zoo is located inside Brandywine Park along the Brandywine River, so there's plenty of room for children to roam and run around afterward. You can also learn about the zoo's many conservation projects, such as monitoring for the American kestrel and working with local wildlife rehabilitators and bird rescuers.

1001 N. Park Dr.
Wilmington, DE 19802
(302) 571-7747, brandywinezoo.org

TIP
Admission rates vary by season, so check the website. The zoo is stroller and wheelchair accessible, with free parking.

STROLL
THE BEST FAMILY-FRIENDLY BOARDWALKS ON THE COAST

You can't go under the boardwalk, but you can stroll, shop, eat, and enjoy the sun and surf to your heart's content along the boards in two of Delaware's famed beach resort towns, Bethany Beach and Rehoboth Beach. The boardwalks are not very long (Bethany's is less than a half mile, and Rehoboth's is a mile), but a lot's packed into that small space just steps away from the sand. Pick up your choice of beach eats from French fries to ice cream, stock up on sandy supplies from boogie boards to sunglasses, and catch free public concerts at the bandstands. (Each town also has a homegrown bookstore for picking up a beach read.) Just watch out for the seagulls flying overhead. They've been known to snatch fries right out of visitors' hands.

LET
YOUR KIDS TAKE THE LEAD
AT THE DELAWARE CHILDREN'S MUSEUM

When the Kahunaville restaurant and bar on Wilmington's Riverfront closed more than a decade ago, it ended up being a major gain for local kids. After years of a nomadic existence, the Delaware Children's Museum (DCM) made the space its permanent home.

At 37,000 square feet, it's not as expansive as the children's museums you might find in bigger cities, but that's actually part of what makes the DCM great. It's easily doable in a day, your children can spend as much time as they like in the exhibits without fear of missing anything, and you'll have no problem keeping track of little ones.

The main entrance area is dominated by a 30-foot-diameter climbing structure called "The Stratosphere." Branching out from the entrance are areas devoted to structures and buildings, nature, the human body, money, and more. Make sure you check out the Tree Pavilion, a hollowed-out 350-year-old sycamore tree originally from nearby Alapocas Woods.

During the warmer months, children will want to check out Riverwalk Mini Golf, an 18-hole course located right behind the museum. If they still aren't tired or if you're looking for something to appease tweens and teens, there's an Altitude Trampoline Park steps away.

550 Justison St.
Wilmington, DE 19801
(302) 654-2340, delawarechildrensmuseum.org

TIP

The DCM doesn't have a restaurant or concession stand on the premises, but shares its free parking lot with several restaurants.

LISTEN TO CONTEMPORARY MUSIC
IN A HISTORIC SETTING

Delaware may be a small state, but its proximity to Philadelphia and Washington makes it easy for national music acts to swing by for a show—and many do, some in an effort to play a concert in each of the 50 states.

Two of the state's grande dames sit less than a half mile apart on downtown Wilmington's main drag, Market Street. You can't miss the brightly glowing lights of the Grand Opera House, which opened in 1871 as a home for the Grand Lodge of the Masons, and in its early heyday as a theatre featured acts including Ethel Barrymore and John Philip Sousa. The theatre eventually became a movie house before falling into disrepair and closing in the late 1960s. Restored, it now hosts more than 80 shows a year. The Delaware Symphony, Delaware Opera, and First State Ballet are also in residence there. The Grand also oversees programming for the Playhouse on Rodney Square, which is located inside the nearby Hotel DuPont and hosts national tours of Broadway favorites.

Down the street, the Queen had a similar rise and fall. It was originally built as a hotel in the early 1800s and was converted to a movie theatre in 1916. It closed in 1959 after a showing of *The House on Haunted Hill* and sat empty for the next 50 years. A local real estate developer bought the crumbling building in 2008, and after a $25 million restoration, the Queen reopened in 2011. It's now managed by national concert booker Live Nation.

The Grand
818 N. Market St.
Wilmington, DE 19801
Tickets: (302) 652-5577
Admin: (302) 658-7897
thegrandwilmington.org

The Queen
500 N. Market St.
Wilmington, DE 19801
(302) 730-3331
thequeenwilmington.com

SEE NATIONAL ACTS
A STONE'S THROW FROM THE BEACHES
AT THE FREEMAN STAGE

Diana Ross, Lyle Lovett, ABBA, and the Steve Miller Band aren't your typical acts to perform in southern Delaware. But since the Freeman Stage opened in 2008, these performers—and a whole host of other crowd-pleasing shows—have been arriving outside tiny Selbyville, playing to appreciative crowds filling the lawn. The venue, part of a nonprofit arts foundation, has a full summer season with an eclectic lineup of shows almost every night, from ballet to Shakespeare and Beatles tribute bands to nationally known comedians like Jim Gaffigan. It's an outdoor venue, so watch the forecast closely. In spring 2020, the Freeman Stage announced a $25 million initiative to expand to 4,400 seats with the addition of the Freeman Arts Pavilion.

31750 Lakeview Dr.
Selbyville, DE 19975
(302) 436-3015
info@freemanfoundation.org
freemanstage.org

TIP

Events advertised as general admission are BYOC (bring your own chair), so make sure it's a comfy one! Those shows tend to fill up quickly. Early arrival is recommended.

SPORTS AND RECREATION

WALK ACROSS THE STATE
ON THE AMERICAN DISCOVERY TRAIL

Walking across the country may be a bit much for most people, but you can sample what it's like to start by walking across Delaware—the eastern end of the 6,800-mile American Discovery Trail. The trail begins on the beach at Cape Henlopen State Park and winds its way across Sussex County, mainly on paved backcountry roads flanked by forests and cornfields.

There are no shoulders on most roads, and the trail crosses three major highways, so hikers should be alert and cautious. It's not a hike for children. It can be isolated, and there are few options along the route for food, water, or bathrooms. The 44.6-mile route winds through downtown Milton and passes by Redden State Forest, which has primitive camping, before it deposits travelers at the Maryland line. If you want to continue, you'll end up at California's Point Reyes National Seashore as just one of a handful of people who've trekked the full trail.

P.O. Box 1514
Front Royal, VA 22630
(800) 663-2387
discoverytrail.org

GET LOST IN A MAZE OF CORN
AT LOCAL FARMS

Forget maze gardens with their sculpted green hedges. Delaware does it one better with corn mazes. Each fall it's practically a rite of passage for families to flock to local farms to navigate their corn mazes and find their way through pathways carved into fields of person-high stalks. The advent of GPS and precision farming has allowed farmers to create elaborate, intricate maze designs when viewed from overhead—think a giant corncob, a map of Delaware, or a sports team logo. Find your way through the pathways of twists, turns, and dead ends, and hear shrieks of laughter and grunts of frustration as others get turned around and discombobulated too. Some farms have mazes that are low-key enough for young children to try by themselves and experience the fun solo!

TIP

There are farms with corn mazes in each county, but call ahead first, as sometimes plans change, and farmers have to skip a year and plant a different crop.

CAST, CATCH, AND RELAX AT THE BEACH
WITH A DAY OF SURF FISHING

Even if you consider yourself a fisherman, casting lines into ponds, rivers, and lakes doesn't prepare you for surf fishing: the ocean experience is vastly different from the inland variety. Each year thousands of fishermen head onto Delaware's designated Atlantic beaches, set up their tall ten- to twelve-foot poles, cast into the surf, and wait for a bite. Leave your freshwater poles and tackle at home, as this requires a completely different mindset. Experts say that you can get a beginner's kit for around $100. You hang out on the beach while your pole does the work, standing upright usually in a piece of PVC pipe stuck into the sand. Look for the birds close to shore. They'll show you where the fish are.

Department of Natural Resources
and Environmental Control
Division of Fish and Wildlife
89 Kings Hwy.
Dover, DE 19904
(302) 739-9910, dnrec.delaware.gov

Delaware Surf Fishing
Local fisherman Rich King has assembled a website full
of resources, fishing spots, fishing reports, news,
and instructional videos perfect for the beginner.
delaware-surf-fishing.com

TIP

Make sure to check in with the state's environmental agency to get a required fisherman's ID number (a FIN). If you're planning to drive onto the beach to fish at the Atlantic state parks, you also have to have a surf fishing permit, and quantities are limited.

CATCH THE RACES,
EQUESTRIAN STYLE

There's nothing quite like the thrill of hooves pounding around the track in a race to the finish. Horse fans have something to enjoy in all three counties in Delaware, with three local racetracks offering regular chances to catch the action. Thoroughbred and Arabian races are held at Delaware Park near Stanton, while harness racing—jockeys riding in carts drawn by Standardbred horses—takes place at both Dover Downs and Harrington Raceway, with simulcast races at all three. Racing in Delaware is tied to casino operations, so you can always try your luck with the slots or a game of blackjack or poker afterward. Racing supports local farms, equipment and feed suppliers, and veterinary services, with a $182 milllion impact.

Delaware Park Racetrack & Slots
777 Delaware Park Blvd.
Wilmington, DE 19804
(800) 41-SLOTS
delawarepark.com

Dover Downs Hotel & Casino
1131 N. DuPont Hwy.
Dover, DE 19901
(302) 674-4600
doverdowns.com

Harrington Raceway & Casino
18500 S. DuPont Hwy.
Harrington, DE 19952
(888) 887-5687
harringtonraceway.com

PADDLE
INTO THE PRIMEVAL
AT TRAP POND STATE PARK

If you like gorgeous scenery and solitude, then paddle into history at Trap Pond State Park, surrounded by shady stands of bald cypress trees. The pond was created in the 1700s to power a sawmill for turning the trees into lumber, but you'll feel that you're millennia back in time in an earlier age when large animals roamed the earth. Spot herons in the shallows, watch turtles sit on cypress knobs, and bring a rod to catch fish (license required). Use your own boat or rent a kayak, canoe, rowboat, or pedal boat during the summer.

People not into paddling can explore the rest of the park, including a nature center, picnic areas, playground, disc golf course, volleyball courts, and hiking trails that travel around the pond's edges. You can use the park as a base for other adventures by camping at a tent site, RV site, or in a cabin or yurt.

33587 Baldcypress Ln.
Laurel, DE 19956
(302) 875-5153, destateparks.com/TrapPond

TIP

Entrance fees are in effect from March 1 to November 30. If you aren't into paddling or have small children, the park runs naturalist-led water tours on a pontoon boat during the summer. Swimming is not permitted.

GET YOUR CLIMB ON
IN THE TREES OR AT THE GYM

Climbing trees is fun for children of all ages. Climbing 50 feet into the very treetops and then sliding on a rope over a pond? That's fun to the extreme.

Located inside Lums Pond State Park, the Go Ape treetop adventure course combines a high-ropes experience with caving ladders, nets, swings, wobbly steps, and five ziplines crossing the pond. The three-hour trial-by-climbing drives your adrenaline through the roof, even though you're connected to safety lines and there's a complete safety briefing before you set foot in the trees. A lower treetop journey course for all ages (children must be at least 3 feet and 3 inches tall) serves as an introductory experience.

Climbers who prefer a more conventional experience can get a day pass, 10-day pass, or membership at the Delaware Rock Gym in Bear, an indoor climbing operation that has both roped climbing and bouldering. If you haven't climbed before, the atmosphere is friendly and professional—no question or concern is too silly—and there are regular introductory classes offered. Come with a buddy to be your belayer!

Go Ape
Lums Pond State Park
1042 Howell School Rd.
Bear, DE 19701
(800) 971-8271
goape.com/location/delaware-bear/

Delaware Rock Gym
520 Carson Dr.
Bear, DE 19701
(302) 838-5850
derockgym.com

TIP

The Go Ape season runs from March to November, and state park entrance fees are charged.

CYCLE A CENTURY
(OR LESS) ALONG COUNTRY ROADS OR CITY STREETS

Cycling is one of Delawareans' favorite hobbies (nearly 60 percent of families count it among their top picks for recreation), and there are plenty of chances for hardcore enthusiasts to feed their inner Greg LeMond. We tallied seven bike tours and similar events up and down the state—from fund-raising rides to fight multiple sclerosis to family-friendly bicycling events—and there are more springing up each year. Each ride offers a great time sharing the camaraderie of your cycling compatriots, and some offer great post-ride fuel, such as the fresh-baked pies at the end of the Amish Country Bike Tour through Kent County's back roads! Check your tires and brakes, grab a water bottle, and put on your helmet, because there's cycling to be done.

Ocean to Bay Bike Tour: April
Sponsored by the Bethany-Fenwick Chamber of Commerce
Distances: 30, 50, 62, and 100 miles
oceantobaybiketour.com

Wilmington Grand Prix: May
A 3.2-mile time trial, amateur races, the Governor's Ride,
and the Delaware Gran Fondo.
wilmgrandprix.com

"Get in Gear" Family Bike Rally: May
Sponsored by Trap Pond Partners
Distance: 5K (the Bob Trail around Trap Pond State Park)
trappondpartners.com

Tour de Sussex: June
Sponsored by Delaware Technical Community College
Distances: 25, 50, and 62 miles
tourdesussex.com

Amish Country Bike Tour: September
Sponsored by Bike Delaware
Distances: 15, 25, 50, 62, and 100 miles
bikede.org

Bike to the Bay: October
Sponsored by the Multiple Sclerosis Society
Distances: 20, 50, 75, 100, 150, and 175 miles
nationalmssociety.org

Dogfish Head IPA (I Pedal A-Lot): October
Distances: 50, 75, and 120 kilometers
dogfish.com

HIKE OR BIKE THE TRAILS,
NO ELEVATION HERE

Delaware is one of the flattest states in the Union—no mountains and few hills. That means if you're into hiking or cycling, you've got a lot of great short trails to stride or ride. Delaware's public trails, spread across state public lands, are perfect for beginners and families. If you're into undespoiled nature, try a loop at Blackbird State Forest near Townsend among huge stands of tall pines. If you want to hear the ocean roar, venture out at Cape Henlopen State Park, where the Atlantic is just steps away but hidden by giant sand dunes.

PADDLE UP TO A LIGHTHOUSE
IN THE DELAWARE BAY

The waters of the Delaware Bay off Cape Henlopen are typically calm and flat—the perfect opportunity for a beginning kayaker building their confidence or an experienced paddler wanting to fly across the water. During the summer season in Cape Henlopen State Park, you can rent a kayak by yourself or go on an organized kayak tour with a group. The best route takes you up to the breakwater and the iconic red Delaware Breakwater Lighthouse, more than 100 years old, that features in countless sunset photos from the Delaware beaches. Paddle past the breakwater's imposing rocks out into the Atlantic for a taste of ocean wave action, and catch a view of the Cape May–Lewes Ferry.

Quest Kayak
(302) 745-2925
questkayak@gmail.com
questkayak.com
Walk-up rentals are located at the fishing pier
at Cape Henlopen State Park, 15099 Cape Henlopen
Drive, Lewes, DE 19958.

RENT A BIKE
FOR RELAXING RESORT CYCLING

There's nothing better than the wind in your hair, the sun on your face, and the scent of sea breeze surrounding you. One of the best ways to get around Delaware's resort beaches is by bicycle. Whether it's cruising up and down the Rehoboth Boardwalk, riding the beaches with a special fat-tired bike, or watching your children pedal around the Quiet Resorts to the south, cycling is a great way to spend the summer at the coast. Many rental shops up and down the area cater to visiting cyclists with quite reasonable rates and service.

Cyclists also have a way to get from Lewes to Rehoboth Beach, which are normally separated by a few miles of busy highway. The Junction and Breakwater Trail is a five-mile crushed-stone rail trail running parallel to Delaware Route 1 between the two towns. It follows the path of the old Penn Central railroad and has interpretive signage and a stopoff behind the Tanger Outlets for a little shopping!

PRACTICE
YOUR MARKSMANSHIP
FOR A FEW BUCKS

For outdoors and hunting enthusiasts, Delaware offers an inexpensive, publicly accessible opportunity to fire away and hone their skills. The Ommelanden Hunter Education Training Center is a bare essentials outdoor range facility with one goal in mind: shooting safely. Shooters can practice trap and skeet shooting, rifle and pistol shooting, and archery for just a few dollars. Archery enthusiasts can send their arrows downrange for just $3 per half-day, while the pistol range is $4 per half hour. While there is no instruction like you might find at a commercial range, the focus is on training and safety, so an initial orientation is required.

1205 River Rd.
New Castle, DE 19720
(302) 382-1074
dnrec.alpha.delaware.gov/fish-wildlife/hunter-education/ommelanden/

TIP

These are simple outdoor ranges with few amenities and portable toilets. Bring water and snacks if you're making a day of it, and wear clothing appropriate for the weather.

FARM ICE CREAM AT HOPKINS FARM CREAMERY (page 2)

PRIME HOOK (page 112)

FORT MILES FIRE CONTROL CENTER (page 139)

AIR MOBILITY COMMAND MUSEUM (page 142)

FIRST STATE NATIONAL HISTORIC PARK OLD STATE HOUSE (page 130)
Photo credit: Divison of Historic and Cultural Affairs

KALMAR NYCKEL (page 124)
Photo credit: Kalmar Nyckel Foundation

GOVERNOR'S CAFE (page 33)

OLD CHRIST CHURCH (page 143)

SCRAPPLE (page 4)

BING'S BAKERY (page 7)

BRANDYWINE PARK (page 106)

CHANGE AND FALL BVT THAT WHI

DELAWARE CHILDREN'S MUSEUM (page 58)

SANDCASTLES (page 108)

WOODBURN (page 144)

CORN MAZES (page 67)

DOLLE'S CANDYLAND (page 8)

WATCH SPORTS.
LOTS OF THEM.

If sports is your thing, Delaware has no end of excitement! Though the tiny state has no major sports teams, we are home to two farm teams in basketball and baseball as well as a professional hockey team. Youth sports are big in the First State, with plenty of opportunities and fields for children to show off their athletic abilities.

Sports at the Beach has 16 baseball fields, 30 outdoor batting cages, a swimming pool, and playgrounds. The DE Turf Sports Complex features 12 fields and a championship stadium, hosting tournaments and lessons in soccer, lacrosse, field hockey, flag football, rugby, and more. For 20 years, southern Delaware has hosted the Senior League Softball World Series each August, featuring some of the nation's best 13- to 16-year-old players. The Centre Ice Arena in Harrington is home to the Delaware Thunder team in the Federal Prospects Hockey League. And the state's two minor league outfits, the Wilmington Blue Rocks baseball and the Delaware Blue Coats basketball team, both play at the Wilmington Riverfront.

Sports at the Beach
22518 Lewes Georgetown Hwy.
Georgetown, DE 19947
(302) 856-7400
sportsatthebeach.com

DE Turf Sports Complex
4000 Bay Rd.
Frederica, DE 19946
(302) 330-TURF
deturf.com

Lower Sussex Little League Complex
34476 Pyle Center Rd.
Frankford, DE 19945
lowersussexlittleleague.com

Delaware Thunder / Centre Ice Arena
644 Fairgrounds Rd.
Harrington, DE 19952
(302) 398-PUCK
delawarethunder.com

Wilmington Blue Rocks
801 Shipyard Dr.
Wilmington, DE 19801
milb.com/wilmington

Delaware Blue Coats / 76ers Fieldhouse
401 Garasches Lane
Wilmington, DE 19801
bluecoats.gleague.nba.com
76ersfieldhouse.com

GET YOUR OUTDOORS FIX CAMPING
AT A PRIME SWEET SPOT

There's nothing more relaxing than kicking back around a campfire, sleeping in a tent or under the stars, and cooking over a stove under a stand of pines. Camping sites are plentiful around Delaware, whether you prefer to do it in a tent, RV, or cabin. There are year-round sites available at five state parks, so if you like the outdoors when snow is on the ground, you're in luck! Campsites are usually located on shaded loop roads with parking at the site or in nearby lots, with electrical and water hookups available at many sites. From your campsite, you can explore the park and go boating, swimming, and hiking or use it as a base for adventuring farther afield into towns and nearby attractions. At Delaware's state forests, there's a different type of camping experience, with primitive tent camping—no indoor shelter, showers, or flush toilets—on offer at Blackbird and Redden state forests. A variety of private campgrounds also specialize in RV sites and have a host of amenities.

TIP
Lums Pond State Park is the official campground for the University of Delaware and offers a discount for Blue Hens fans during fall football season.

Delaware State Parks
Reservations: (877) 987-2757
destateparks.com

Delaware Forest Service
(302) 698-4547
agriculture.delaware.gov/forest-service/

Delaware Campgrounds
visitdelaware.com/where-to-stay/campground/

SKIMBOARD WITH THE PROS
AT DEWEY BEACH

Each summer the world's best skimboarders—or skimmers—gather in Delaware to catch the waves for the Zap Pro/Am World Championships. Skimboarding is similar to surfing but involves a small, finless board—and lots of skill and stunts. Skimboarders try to outdo each other with spins, kicks, and other tricks while the crashing waves take them back into shore, and Dewey Beach is a prime skimboarding spot. It's been called the second largest skim event in the world, with the largest at Laguna Beach, California. Every August local skim shop Alley-Oop sponsors the free Summer Vibes Fest, which includes the skimboarding championships and also highlights skateboarding, art, and music. The 2019 pro skim champion hailed from Rio de Janeiro, Brazil.

1904 Coastal Hwy.
Dewey Beach, DE 19971
(302) 227-7087
info@alleyoopskim.com

TIP
Alley-Oop also offers beginning lessons in skimboarding, surfing, and skateboarding.

WALK AMONG THE DUNES
AT CAPE HENLOPEN

Sand dunes are the guardians of the Atlantic coastline. They protect inland areas from being eroded by the power of the thundering ocean waves. Beach visitors to Delaware's Cape Henlopen State Park, which is to say most of the park's visitors, usually see only the front of the dunes, which take the brunt of the wind and wave action. But a walk on the park's trails will take you through the remarkable natural ecosystems that exist a short distance from the ocean—pine trees, deer, bogs, snakes, and marshes—and even take you to the Great Dune, rising above the Atlantic. Photography enthusiasts will especially love the natural environment and photo opportunities.

15099 Cape Henlopen Dr.
Lewes, DE
(302) 645-8983
destateparks.com/Beaches/CapeHenlopen

PADDLE
THE NANTICOKE RIVER
LIKE CAPTAIN JOHN SMITH

In 1608, Captain John Smith—yes, the one of Pocahontas lore—went on a voyage of exploration that took him up the Nanticoke River, reaching the junction with Broad Creek, near Laurel. Today, paddlers can travel the same route along the Nanticoke, experiencing stunning natural sights including bald eagles, marshes, and woodlands. Canoers and kayakers can easily put in at one of several public launch ramps in Delaware (at Phillips Landing outside Laurel, or the Seaford Boat Ramp and Nanticoke River Marina in Seaford) or in Maryland and explore to their hearts' content. (Some may charge launch fees, so research before you go.) Know your limits, though; the Nanticoke is actively plied by barge and tugboat traffic, and currents can sweep you off course.

Captain John Smith Chesapeake
National Historic Trail
nps.gov/cajo/index.htm

Nanticoke Watershed Alliance
113 Old Ocean Gateway
P.O. Box 111
Vienna, MD 21869
(410) 430-3273, nanticokeriver.org

TIP
A boaters' guide to the entire Captain John Smith Chesapeake National Historic Trail was penned by author John Page Williams, a naturalist with the Chesapeake Bay Foundation, and includes a wealth of history and travel advice.

DID YOU KNOW?

The Nanticoke Watershed Alliance is
an umbrella group of diverse interests—
environmental, industry, agriculture, and
governmental—working to conserve the
725,000-acre Nanticoke watershed across two
states. Volunteer creek watchers monitor
the health of local tributaries each year.

WATCH
THE SEASONS CHANGE
AT BRANDYWINE PARK

Wilmington's very first city park was established in 1886 along the banks of Brandywine Creek. The park still retains an old-fashioned vibe, even on a warm summer weekend when it's full of joggers, dog walkers, fishermen, and picnickers.

There's something at Brandywine Park for everyone: the approximately 178 acres include walking paths, picnic areas, a playground, athletic fields, a stadium, and since 1904, the Brandywine Zoo. As the walking path meanders along the Brandywine, you'll pass by waterfalls, historic buildings, and bridges, including the commanding arches of the underside of a span of Interstate 95. In the springtime, the cherry blossoms create a breathtaking scene on either side of the Josephine Fountain, which has recently reopened after a five-year restoration project. In the late summer, this stretch of park is also the site of the Brandywine Festival of the Arts. Nearby, the Jasper Crane Rose Garden contains hundreds of bushes that bloom in red, pink, yellow, and peach in the spring, summer, and fall.

Fall leaves will bring out leaf peepers, but the park is also a sight to behold in the winter after a snowfall, when it's mostly quiet, and you may feel that the scenery was put there just for you.

1080 N. Park Dr.
Wilmington, DE 19806
destateparks.com/Wilmington

TIP

Part of the Northern Delaware Greenway Trail connects Brandywine Park with Alapocas Run State Park. Along that stretch, you'll see an old quarry that has been repurposed as a climbing area as well as parts of an abandoned mill.

DID YOU KNOW?

The park was created with the consultation of Frederick Law Olmsted, who designed New York's Central Park.

FEEL LIKE ROYALTY
BY BUILDING A SANDCASTLE
ON THE BEACH

It's not unusual to take a walk on one of Delaware's beaches at the end of a long summer day and see the coastline dotted with sandcastles, ranging from simple structures to elaborate palaces.

Both Rehoboth Beach and Delaware Seashore State Park hold annual summer sandcastle contests where you can see structures created by professionals. But it's easy enough to build a sandy beach home of your own. Just bring some cups and utensils from home or pick up some plastic buckets from a store on your way and start experimenting once you hit the beach.

If you happen to be on Lewes Beach in August, keep an eye out for the Sandcastle Lady, a beachgoer who builds fancy castles of her own and is happy to lend out molding materials and advice to fellow visitors, especially children. She shares photos online of her creations and those made by the people she meets.

TIP

Lewes Beach calms down considerably after around 6:00 p.m. even on the busiest summer weekends. Come to watch the sunset, swim, and build castles without having to brave the crowds.

WATCH
PREHISTORIC CREATURES SWARM THE SHORES BY THE LIGHT OF THE MOON

Let's get this out of the way: horseshoe crabs aren't true crabs but an ancient species hundreds of millions of years old that come up every spring and summer out of the Delaware Bay to spawn on the beaches. Think thousands of hard-shelled creatures scrabbling their way from the waters onto the sand, doing their business, and sliding back into the bay. The eggs they lay are prime food for migratory shorebirds. Watching them spawn is an awe-inspiring experience, especially at night. Time your visit to the new and full moons and at the overnight high tide for the best viewing. Prime sites are at Pickering Beach, Kitts Hummock, and Slaughter Beach. You can also volunteer with the Delaware National Estuarine Research Reserve for a spawning survey to count the crabs and contribute to the body of scientific knowledge about these fascinating creatures!

TIP
For safety, bring a flashlight, but out of politeness to other visitors and bayside residents, keep your voices and lights low.

HIKE
ACROSS DELAWARE
ON THE BANKS OF A CANAL

You know Delaware is tiny, but just how tiny? One particularly skinny part is just 15 miles wide, and it's been made perfect for a stroll. The Michael N. Castle Chesapeake and Delaware Canal Trail, named after a former governor, goes 8.7 miles through wildlife preserves along the north side of the canal, connecting Delaware City and the Summit North Marina. Walkers can get a great view of the canal, the boat traffic, and the natural surroundings of the preserve. You can do it out-and-back and double your miles or use a car at either end. It's also great for cyclists.

If your timing is right, you can join a bunch of other hiking and walking enthusiasts traversing that width at the same time. Every winter the Wilmington Trail Club holds the Hike across Delaware, which marked its 25th anniversary in 2019. The group goes east from Chesapeake City to Delaware City, and November weather usually makes for a brisk and pleasant walk.

SEE BIRDS
FROM ALL OVER THE WORLD
AT STUNNING WILDLIFE REFUGES

Some of the best bird-watching opportunities in the world are right here in Delaware. Going birding is a unique experience unlike any other outdoor activity, involving casual strolling, fresh air, and quiet, and some very keen eyes (or good binoculars!). Two key spots are the state's national wildlife refuges along the Delaware coast, Prime Hook (near Milton) and Bombay Hook (near Smyrna)—more than 25,000 acres of pristine habitat. Migratory birds heading north and south along the Atlantic Flyway often stop in Delaware, making it a fantastic spot to spot birds you don't normally see here. (There's a reason that the American Birding Association moved to Delaware in 2014!) Walk piney trails or hike the marshes to get a glimpse of some new birds to add to your life list. To get started, the refuges even have a great checklist of what birds you can see at certain times of the year. The Delmarva Birding Weekends are special events throughout the year that draw together birding enthusiasts from all over. And for non-birders, the hiking and photo opportunities along the trails are astounding.

Prime Hook National Wildlife Refuge 11978 Turkle Pond Rd. Milton, DE 19968 (302) 684-8419 fws.gov/refuge/prime_hook/	Bombay Hook National Wildlife Refuge 2591 Whitehall Neck Rd. Smyrna, DE 19977 (302) 653-9345 fws.gov/refuge/bombay_hook/

TIP

Prime Hook is free, but Bombay Hook charges an entrance fee (cash or check only). It's $4 per car for a single visit or $12 for an annual refuge pass, so if you know you're coming back, that's a bargain.

CULTURE AND HISTORY

SET FOOT
ON A CIVIL WAR ISLAND PRISON

Located on the charmingly named Pea Patch Island, Fort Delaware was built in 1859 in the center of the Delaware Bay to guard the important Wilmington and Philadelphia ports. During the Civil War, the Union fort became a prisoner-of-war camp to hold Confederate soldiers. It housed more than 12,000 Southern POWs at one time.

Today, it's one of Delaware's state parks, though with limited seasonal access (open from the end of April through September). You ride a ferry there, leaving from Delaware City, and disembark to be greeted by a team of costumed living history interpreters who share tales of grand escapes and life at the fort for Union soldiers and the Confederate prisoners they guarded in 1864. The stone walls can talk too: in the fall, join a special paranormal tour! Fort Delaware's ghostly tales have been showcased on *Ghost Hunters* and other TV shows.

Ticket Office	Park Office
45 Clinton St.	108 N. Reedy Point Rd.
Delaware City, DE	Delaware City, DE
Tickets: (877) 98-PARKS	(302) 834-7941

destateparks.com/History/FortDelaware

TIP

Wear closed-toed shoes, not sandals or flip-flops. Visitors are asked to step onto "wet biomats," which will prevent the spread of a fungal disease that kills bats (but is harmless to humans).

IN THE ARDENS,
COME FOR THE ARTS, STAY FOR THE STORYBOOK ATMOSPHERE

Not many communities can say they were founded on the principles of an obscure economic theory from an 1800s journalist. Delaware boasts three of them, just north of the city of Wilmington proper.

The history of "the Ardens," as the villages of Arden, Ardencroft, and Ardentown are collectively known, is tied to a then popular "single-tax" political reform put forward by journalist Henry George. Today, the Ardens are largely known as an artist colony and are the quaint backdrop for year-round plays and musical performances. Each village is home to only a few hundred people, and open space abounds.

Highly active local "gilds," or community clubs, organize things like live music, a library, folk dancing, poetry, and gardening. The Gild Hall, owned by the Arden Club, plays host to many events, with an outdoor amphitheatre for elaborate theatrical performances. And the end of August always draws a very large crowd of outsiders to bid farewell to the summer with the Arden Fair.

2126 The Highway
Arden, DE 19810
(302) 475-3126, ardenclub.org

TIP
Bring your camera and walking shoes for some excellent photo opportunities.

WRAP YOUR ARMS
AROUND THE BIGGEST TREES
IN DELAWARE

Hunting for big trees can be exhilarating and educational at the same time. Delaware has made it easy with a regularly updated guide from the state forest service, which documents the state's widest and tallest trees by species. Many of the trees are on private property; ask the landowner's permission to go on their land.

The tallest and widest trees in the state are both located in northern Delaware. The tallest soars 173 feet high, a yellow poplar on the campus of the Winterthur estate in Wilmington—or about 24 Shaquille O'Neals stacked on top of each other. It will take a few friends to get your arms around the state's widest tree, a non-native zelkova tree in Greenville more than 27 feet around.

Big Trees of Delaware
Delaware Forest Service
2320 S. DuPont Hwy.
Dover, DE 19901
(302) 698-4500, delawaretrees.com/bigtrees/

DID YOU KNOW?
Hagley Museum in Wilmington is home to 14 of the trees in the Big Trees book.

STROLL AROUND
SCENIC GARDENS AND GUNPOWDER MILLS AT HAGLEY MUSEUM

It's said that the wealthy du Pont family built Delaware, and there's no better way to learn about this family's heritage and impact than by visiting the historic gunpowder mills that were the start of the iconic company's business. What surprises some visitors is that the site of the mills along the Brandywine River was also home to the du Pont family. The company founder, E. I. du Pont, built his mansion above the powder mills, and you can visit both with a stop at the Hagley Museum & Library. Strolling through the house and gardens gives visitors insight into the lives of American business royalty, and walking through the powder works provides a glimpse into the working conditions of the men who ran the waterwheels, steam engines, turbines, and stone quarry that produced gunpowder and later blasting powder and dynamite.

200 Hagley Creek Rd.
Wilmington, DE 19807
(302) 658-2400
hagley.org

TIP
Try to plan your visit for the spring, when the du Pont gardens are in bloom. It's well worth it to see the results of E. I. du Pont's true passion.

LEARN ABOUT OLD-TIME HEROES
AT A HISTORIC LIFESAVING STATION

In 1876, to help save the lives of sailors cast into the Atlantic after shipwrecks along the coast, the federal government built the Indian River Lifesaving Station along a stretch of Sussex County beach. The heroic rescuers risked life and limb using primitive equipment to retrieve the victims of the surf. Today, the station still stands as a museum and parks center rather than an active rescue operation. It has been restored to the way it looked in 1905 and plays host to a great number of educational programs and activities for the whole family—nighttime lantern tours, shipwreck stories, dissecting squid, making sea glass jewelry, and more. One of the summertime highlights is a reenactment and demonstration of the "breeches buoy," which helped rescue shipwreck victims. It's also a popular site for weddings, receptions, and meetings, and has a gift shop with plenty of trinkets and educational materials.

25039 Coastal Hwy.
Rehoboth Beach, DE 19971
(302) 227-6991
destateparks.com/History/IRLifeSavingStation

PEER INSIDE
THE WORKINGS
OF A HISTORIC MILL

For more than 200 years, a mill has stood on the banks of Abbott's Pond outside Milford, using the power of the water to cut lumber and grind food. It began as a sawmill in 1795 and was converted to a grist mill in 1810, running to 1960.

Today, the mill still operates for the public on selected days, run by the Delaware Nature Society as a part of the Abbott's Mill Nature Center. Nothing is ground, but the mill still runs to show visitors how the high technology of the 1800s worked. Stepping inside the yellow building is a journey into a time when thick, rough wooden beams, giant stones, and the rush of water turned barley, wheat, and corn into meal for families all over the area. Back in those days, mills were commonplace in the state, given Delaware's coastal access to shipping.

15411 Abbott's Pond Rd.
Milford, DE 19953
(302) 422-0847
delawarenaturesociety.org/centers/abbotts-mill-nature-center/

TIP

Guided tours of the mill usually run on select Saturdays March through November. Nature Society members enter free; nonmembers pay a small fee.

RIDE
THE OLDEST OPERATING FERRY IN THE US

The tiny community of Woodland sits on the western bank of the Nanticoke River. On the other side is a road that leads into the town of Laurel. There has never been a bridge crossing the river at this point—only a ferry dating back to the 1700s. Today, the Woodland Ferry is the oldest operating ferry in the nation.

Riding the ferry, which is guided by a cable so that it doesn't go off course or get pulled downstream during the 400-foot trip, is a journey of just a few minutes that calls that history to mind. It's not a giant ferry like the Cape May–Lewes ships that crisscross the Delaware Bay, but a small six-vehicle vessel that carries you securely floating just a short distance above the waters of the Nanticoke. It makes about 45,000 trips a year, carrying about 225 cars and trucks per day plus cyclists and pedestrians, and the trip is absolutely free.

7:00 a.m.–6:30 p.m. daily, year-round;
closed Thursday mornings for maintenance
deldot.gov/Programs/woodland_ferry/index.shtml

DID YOU KNOW?
The ferry occasionally undergoes maintenance, so check online to make sure it's operating before you leave.

SEE ART
ON THE CUTTING EDGE
AT THE CONTEMPORARY

A non-collecting museum, The Delaware Contemporary features more than 24 annual exhibitions of regionally, nationally, and internationally recognized artists, and since there are no permanent holdings, you'll always see something new when you visit. Many of the pieces on display in the seven galleries are also for sale, and sales benefit both the artist and the museum.

Founded in (1979, The Delaware Contemporary's 33,000-square-foot space on Wilmington's Riverfront is a home for artists on several levels. It has 26 on-site art studios occupied by local painters, photographers, and sculptors. You can visit many of the studios on the first Friday of each month during Wilmington's Art Loop. A shuttle that starts and ends at the Delaware Contemporary will also take you to other galleries throughout the city.

The Delaware Contemporary also offers an "art fitness" series that offers emerging artists the chance to develop their professional skill set, including review sessions with the museum's curators and workshops on art pricing.

200 S. Madison St.
Wilmington, DE 19801
decontemporary.org

TIP
Admission is always free (though there is a suggested donation).

TRAVEL ON A REPLICA
OF A 1600s-ERA SAILING SHIP

If you're a fan of maritime adventures and seafaring tales, then you don't want to miss a ride on the *Kalmar Nyckel*, Delaware's replica of a 17th-century Dutch ship that led colonial expeditions to the New World. It's an impressive sight to see from shore going up and down the Delaware Bay and even more awe-inducing to see the sails fill from the deck and feel it cut through the water. From its berth in Wilmington, the tall ship sails as far south as Virginia and as far north as New England every year between May and October. You can book a regular sail of up to two and a half hours, a special pirate-themed sail, or a kid-focused pirate adventure. You can also charter the ship for private sails.

From December to April, when the ship is up for maintenance, enthusiasts can still take a dockside tour most Saturdays. Its museum, the Copeland Maritime Center, features exhibits and educational displays about the history and science of sailing.

Kalmar Nyckel Shipyard / Copeland Maritime Center
1124 E. Seventh St.
Wilmington, DE 19801
(302) 429-7447
kalmarnyckel.org

TIP

If your visit leaves you having caught the sailing bug, join the more than 200 volunteers who fill vital roles in the ship's operations, including sailing on its crew.

DID YOU KNOW?

The first *Kalmar Nyckel*, built in 1625, was the flagship of a 1638 Dutch expedition that founded the New Sweden colony. She crossed the Atlantic Ocean four times and was likely sunk in 1652 in a war against the English. The modern replica was launched in 1997.

HEAR THE HISTORY
OF SOUND COME ALIVE
AT JOHNSON VICTROLA MUSEUM

The late 1800s and early 1900s were a period of innovation in sound recording, and a chief pioneer was Delaware-born inventor Eldridge Reeves Johnson. In 1902, he founded the Victor Talking Machine Company, which produced Victrolas—phonographs targeting the consumer market. Johnson also famously used the image of the dog Nipper from an 1899 painting to promote Victrola sales. This free museum is tucked away in an unassuming brick building on a side street in downtown Dover, the state capital, but inside it has a wide selection of Victrolas. Exhibits and displays showcase Johnson's accomplishments and the company's history, including old phonographs, horns, Nipper statues and artwork, and records—and Johnson's posthumous 1985 Grammy Award.

375 S. New St.
Dover, DE 19904
(302) 739-3262
history.delaware.gov/jvm_main/

EXPLORE
A PEACEFUL 1700s VILLAGE

To most drivers in northern Delaware, Odessa is known as part of the "MOT" area, spanning the communities of Middletown, Odessa, and Townsend. Today, history welcomes you to tiny Odessa, thanks to the work of dedicated preservationists keeping the dream alive. In the 1700s, the community was a port called Cantwell's Bridge; today, you can dine at the regional-fare Cantwell's Tavern, originally a hotel built in the 1820s, where the brunch is a must-try (especially the omelet).

Lovers of architecture and art will have a lot to appreciate. There are five historic buildings to explore on 30 acres of gardens and lawns, featuring artwork, 18th-century furniture pieces, a sanctuary for enslaved people seeking freedom, and fine crafts. Throughout the year, the village offers workshops and presentations, including how to cook on an 18th-century hearth. The highlight of the year is the holiday tour every December, attracting many visitors to stroll the streets and admire the decorations.

Historic Odessa Foundation
P.O. Box 697
Odessa, DE 19730
(302) 378-4119
info@historicodessa.org
historicodessa.org

Cantwell's Tavern
109 Main St.
Odessa, DE 19730
(302) 376-0600
info@cantwells-tavern.com
cantwells-tavern.com

SEE THE HULL
OF A SHIPWRECK FROM THE 1700s

Sunken treasure tales always spark the imagination. Tales of gold going down with the HMS *De Braak* spurred recovery efforts beginning after she sank off Cape Henlopen in 1798, but it was not until 1984 that the wreckage was discovered. Today, the State of Delaware owns 20,000 objects recovered from the ship as well as part of the hulk itself. Only a few gold coins and a ring were found, but the history that the ship has taught is invaluable.

Since the ship was raised in 1986, preservationists have worked to prevent the hull from deteriorating, keeping it under a constant spray of water in a nondescript building inside Cape Henlopen State Park. Each year small groups of visitors get to see what remains of the hull—a bit of an eerie experience, knowing that the damaged timbers and copper plates spent nearly two centuries lying on the ocean floor holding the remains of the ship's crew. (The crew is buried on the grounds of the museum; Captain James Drew is buried at St. Peter's Episcopal Church in Lewes.)

102 Kings Hwy.
Lewes, DE 19958
(302) 645-1148
history.delaware.gov

TIP

Tours run June through September, and space is limited. The program begins at the Zwaanendael Museum, with participants then taken by van to the hull preservation building. Bring a bottle of water and use the restroom before you leave.

DELVE INTO
DELAWARE HISTORY
AT OUR NATIONAL PARK

For decades, Delaware lacked a national park. That changed with the creation of the First State National Historic Park—seven locations across the state that highlight Delaware's heritage and natural wonders. You can visit them all in a day, but it's advised to take your time and do each in turn to soak up the history.

Much of the park is in northern Delaware—Fort Christina, where the first Swedish and Finnish settlers landed in the New World; a 1699-era church called the oldest church in the country that still holds worshippers; a 1,100-acre natural preserve with 18 miles of trails; and the 1732 courthouse that was the colony's original capitol.

In central and southern Delaware, visit the Green where Delaware's delegates ratified the Constitution, the plantation owned by Founding Father John Dickinson, and a 1665 home in coastal Lewes that survived raids by the English.

TIP

There is no central visitor center for the park.
Most of the sites are managed by partner
nonprofits and government agencies, so check
out the details and call ahead to the
specific sites if you have questions.

Beaver Valley
nps.gov/frst/planyourvisit/beaver-valley.htm

Fort Christina
1110 East Seventh St.
Wilmington, DE 19801
Open Memorial Day to Labor Day
nps.gov/frst/planyourvisit/fort-christina.htm

Old Swedes Historic Site
606 N. Church St.
Wilmington, DE 19801
Open March to December; January and February
are by appointment only
nps.gov/frst/planyourvisit/old-swedes-church.htm

New Castle Court House
211 Delaware St.
New Castle, DE 19720
(302) 323-4453
nps.gov/frst/planyourvisit/new-castle-court-house.htm

The Green
25 The Green
Dover, DE 19901
(302) 739-9194
The Green itself is open year-round, with educational tours
available through Delaware State Parks' First State Heritage
Park Monday to Saturday.
nps.gov/frst/planyourvisit/the-green-dover.htm

John Dickinson Plantation
340 Kitts Hummock Rd.
Dover, DE 19901
(302) 739-3277
nps.gov/frst/planyourvisit/john-dickinson-plantation.htm

Ryves Holt House
218 Second St.
Lewes, DE 19958
(302) 645-7670
Open end of May to early September
nps.gov/frst/planyourvisit/ryves-holt-house.htm

EXPLORE
UNDERWATER TREASURES
RECOVERED FROM THE DEEP

When the Nuestra Senora de Atocha went down in a storm in 1622, about 260 people drowned, and its cargo of gold, silver, jewelry, and precious gems was lost off the Florida coast. More than 360 years later, the riches were found by treasure hunter Mel Fisher. Today, visitors to Delaware can see more than $4 million in artifacts on display at the Treasures of the Sea exhibit, an intimate series of educational and awe-inspiring displays of silver ingots, cannons, gold coins, emeralds, and other items. In addition to the artifacts, there is a video and life-size photos about the search, a shipwreck diorama, and a gift shop. The museum, located in the library at Delaware Technical Community College, draws a few thousand visitors a year, so chances are good that you'll have the exhibit largely to yourself.

21199 College Dr. (GPS), 21179 College Dr. (Mailing)
Georgetown, DE 19947
(302) 259-6150
treasures@dtcc.edu
treasuresofthesea.org

DID YOU KNOW?

Like many people, you're probably wondering why a bunch of 1600s Spanish treasure and artifacts lost off Florida are on display in southern Delaware. Local businessman Melvin Joseph Sr., of Georgetown, was a financial backer of the Fisher exhibition, and donated some of his share of the treasure for the public exhibit.

SHAKE HANDS
WITH A US SENATOR

As a state with only three counties and fewer than one million residents, politics in Delaware has a small-town feel—even in the state's largest city. Voters here know their elected officials intimately, refer to them by their first names, and aren't afraid to call them up at a moment's notice to complain about a pothole. Legislators can bump into their constituents at the mall, in the frozen food aisle, or on the next elliptical at the YMCA. Smart politicians have even been known to turn waiting in line into a campaign stop, like Delaware's winningest campaigner, US Senator Tom Carper, who's been known to go up and down the queue shaking hands in line at the grocery store. It must work, too: Carper has been state treasurer, congressman, governor, and senator, and hasn't lost a race since 1976. The best place to shake a politician's hand outside of election season is every summer at the Delaware State Fair, which attracts everyone who wants to be someone.

VISIT
A LARGER-THAN-LIFE MURAL
OF STATE HISTORY

Jack Lewis was one of the region's great homegrown artists. A native of nearby Baltimore, he was part of a Delaware Civilian Conservation Corps crew during the Great Depression and documented the work through sketches and paintings. As a teacher after World War II, Lewis also traveled the state painting murals that chronicled local and state history. One on display at Delaware Technical Community College in Georgetown showcases the historic Return Day event, where politicians literally bury a hatchet. Another can be seen on the side of an antique store in his adopted town of Bridgeville. Others were destroyed over the years as buildings were demolished, but a wonderful example was preserved by the Bridgeville Public Library when it moved from an old church into a brand-new building; the mural is on display in the children's room. Lewis's most visible murals can be seen from the visitors' balconies in Dover's Legislative Hall, the building that houses the Delaware General Assembly. Lewis passed away in 2012 at age 99.

EXPERIENCE
THE PAST FIRSTHAND
BY LIVING HISTORY

As the First State, Delaware has seen a lot of history come its way and has many reenactors, historical sites, and programs that turn the past into the present through living history opportunities. The most notable is at Fort Delaware, where costumed presenters in heavy wool costumes—even in the summer heat—tell what it was like to live and work during the Civil War. You can find living history specialists giving tours and demonstrations at the Dickinson Plantation, First State Heritage Park, and the Delaware Agricultural Museum and Village. In coastal Lewes, the historical society showcases a maritime living history festival to teach about three centuries of maritime and naval heritage. And there are occasional events with active Revolutionary War and Civil War reenactment groups around the state.

Delaware Agricultural
Museum and Village
866 N. DuPont Hwy.
Dover, DE 19901
(302) 734-1618
info.damv@verizon.net
agriculturalmuseum.org

Lewes Historical Society
110 Shipcarpenter St.
Lewes, DE 19958
(302) 645-7670
info@historiclewes.org
historiclewes.org

SALUTE
THE GREATEST GENERATION WITH A VISIT TO FORT MILES

Once home to 2,500 soldiers, Fort Miles has a special place in World War II history—a military base built amid dunes and pine trees, with gun batteries and the iconic fire control towers that dot the state's Atlantic coastline. Today, the area is part of Cape Henlopen State Park, with a museum, barracks buildings, and interpretive programs that guide visitors through both local and wartime history. Interpreters also hold regular nighttime lantern tours of Battery 519 for an atmospheric twist. Costumed reenactors portray both US soldiers and German naval personnel at special events, including the simulated surrender of a German U-boat's crew, an event that actually took place at what is now the park's fishing pier in 1945.

Fort Miles / Cape Henlopen State Park
15099 Cape Henlopen Dr.
Lewes, DE 19958
(302) 644-5007
destateparks.com/FortMiles

TIP

Access to Battery 519 is only available through guided tours, and the museum is only available through tours and open houses, so check the park's program schedule before stopping by.

EXPERIENCE GLOBAL CULTURE
AT HERITAGE FESTIVALS

Originally settled by the Swedes, Delaware has become a microcosm of the greater United States (once heralded for its ability to pick the winning presidential candidate in a long string of elections). Today, many diverse cultural, religious, ethnic, and racial groups contribute to its strength and diversity, and visitors and locals alike can gain an appreciation of those contributions at one of many local festivals, celebrating everyone from the First Nations peoples represented by the Nanticoke tribe to Italian and Korean immigrants. Nosh on delicious traditional foods, learn about cultural arts and dancing, and study up on your history and heritage.

TIP
These festivals are typically outdoor extravaganzas over a day or a weekend. Check the weather forecast, bring cash, wear comfortable shoes, and carry a water bottle.

St. Anthony's Italian Festival: June
Wilmington
Italian culture
stanthonysfestival.com

Polish Festival: October
Wilmington
Polish heritage
sthedwigde.org/66

Holy Trinity Greek Festival: June
Wilmington
Greek culture
greekfestde.com

Delaware Saengerbund Oktoberfest: September
Newark
German heritage
delawaresaengerbund.org

The August Quarterly Festival: August
Wilmington
African-American history and culture
augustquarterly.org

The Nanticoke Indian Powwow: September
Millsboro
nanticokeindians.org/page/what-powwow

TOUR HISTORIC AIRCRAFT
ON AN AIR FORCE BASE

Walk down the aisle of a former Air Force One, experience the cramped cockpit of a C-141B Starlifter cargo plane, or sit in the pilot's seat of a Vietnam-era Huey helicopter. If you've ever wanted to do any of those or have a passion for historic aircraft, don't overlook Delaware's Air Mobility Command Museum, located at Dover Air Force Base. The museum's collection includes WWII cloth survival maps, Cold War first aid gear, and a WWI pilot's logbook. But the true highlight is Open Cockpit Day, offered several times each year, when the public can walk into and explore the restored and preserved aircraft, including a KB-50J Superfortress refueler and a giant C-5 Galaxy cargo plane.

Air Mobility Command Museum
1301 Heritage Rd.
Dover Air Force Base, DE 19902
(302) 677-5938
amcmuseum.org

TIP
Admission and parking are always free!

WORSHIP AS IN
THE REVOLUTIONARY ERA

To sit in a wooden pew inside Old Christ Church, located just outside Laurel, is to share in the worship experience of ordinary Colonial-era Americans. The red-sided, pinewood Episcopal church remains as it was in 1772—no electricity, no plumbing, no heating or cooling. Pews are in the box style, not open seating as we're used to today. The church is open during the warmer months for select Sunday services and for special events, such as a Blessing of the Animals, Christmas caroling, or a Thanksgiving service. Tours are available after services by contacting the Old Christ Church League.

Chipmans Pond Rd. and Christ Church Rd.
Laurel, DE 19956
facebook.com/OldChristChurchLeague/

TIP
If you're attending a winter event, bring your warmest clothing and blankets!

EXPLORE
THE HISTORIC GOVERNOR'S MANSION

The house known as Woodburn, situated on a quiet Dover street a few blocks from the state capitol building, has been the official home of Delaware's governors for just over 50 years. A few have lived there full-time, while most have used it as a ceremonial and official residence for special meetings, dinners, and public events. The house itself dates back to 1798 and has been home to a US senator, farmers, a judge, and several doctors. There is a "Wall of First Ladies," a parlor room with historical artifacts, and a great hall often used for dining. Woodburn's gardens and grounds have been enhanced by subsequent governors, with special trees planted by succeeding officeholders. When Governor Michael N. Castle married Jane DiSabatino during the final year of his term, they planted "Bride and Groom" American holly trees behind the house. Tours are available from 8:30 a.m. to 4:00 p.m. Monday to Friday by appointment.

151 Kings Hwy. SW
Dover, DE 19901
(302) 739-5656
woodburn.delaware.gov

GET A BIRD'S-EYE VIEW
IN ROCKFORD PARK

A more than 100-year-old stone tower is the centerpiece of Rockford Park, one of Wilmington's oldest. The park, a large grassy meadow that slopes upward to overlook the Brandywine River, was the brainchild of local philanthropist and conservationist William Poole Bancroft, and in 1889, he donated 59 acres of his own land to establish it. Today, the park includes an off-leash area for dogs and space for hiking, picnicking, grilling, and a concert series during the summer. Every spring the park is home to the 100-year-old Wilmington Flower Market, which celebrates the season with plant sales, food, music, and games.

The 75-foot Rockford Tower was originally built in 1901 as both a water tower and observation point. A winding staircase leads to an observation deck with distinctive arched windows that look out on Wilmington and the surrounding area. While you're on the ground, keep an eye out for the sundial affixed to one side of the tower. The tower is open for tours on summer Sundays and during Monday evening summer concerts.

1021 W. 18th St.
Wilmington, DE 19806
destateparks.com/Wilmington

EXPERIENCE BEAUTY BOTH INSIDE AND OUT
AT WINTERTHUR

Collector and horticulturist Henry Francis du Pont combined both his loves when he opened his childhood home Winterthur, pronounced "winter-tour," to the public in 1951. The 175-room house is now a museum dedicated to the decorative arts and furnished with some of Winterthur's collection of almost 90,000 pieces of furniture, ceramics, glass, metals, textiles, paintings, and prints, including those from du Pont's own collection. There are several themed house tours, including one designed specifically for young children and the popular Yuletide tour during the Christmas holidays. The adjacent galleries are home to more objects from the permanent collection, but also host traveling exhibitions.

After gawking at the opulence inside, visitors can venture outside to wander the 1,000-acre grounds, which feature rolling hills, streams, meadows, forests, and a 60-acre landscaped garden. Tram tours are available, but if you're up to it, the best way to enjoy it is to walk. Springtime brings the annual Point-to-Point steeplechase, where you can enjoy a day of horse racing and some of the most elegant tailgating you've ever seen.

5105 Kennett Pike
Winterthur, DE 19735
(302) 888-4600, winterthur.org

TIP

Purchase tickets and reserve specialty tours in advance, particularly during the popular Christmas season.

DID YOU KNOW?

Winterthur is also a living laboratory and research facility: in partnership with the University of Delaware, the museum sponsors well-reguarded graduate programs in material culture and art conservation. Individual scholars can also apply for research fellowships.

SEE THE STARS
AT MOUNT CUBA OBSERVATORY

Delaware's only public observatory, Mount Cuba is an all-volunteer organization that is home to professional and amateur astronomers alike. The observatory's 24-inch diameter refracting telescope is used for international astronomical projects, studies, and research through a working relationship with the University of Delaware.

At the same time, Mt. Cuba is also a learning lab for the general public. On selected Monday nights, the observatory is open for public nights offering tours, planetarium programs, and lectures on astronomical topics. When sky conditions are right, the observatory is open for viewing planets, the moon, and other objects in the sky through the smaller 4.5-inch refracting telescope. Family nights are scheduled from late spring to early fall on Friday nights and focus on teaching kids 6 to 12 about astronomy.

1610 Hillside Mill Rd.
Wilmington, DE 19807
(302) 654-6407, mountcuba.org

TIP

Make a day of it by visiting the nearby Mt. Cuba Center, a botanical garden known for its wildflowers.

VIEW FAMOUS ART
AND MAKE SOME OF YOUR OWN
AT THE DELAWARE ART MUSEUM

Brightly colored, flowerlike blown glass by artist Dale Chihuly adorns the bridge linking the second floors of two wings of Wilmington's Delaware Art Museum. It's probably the most visible piece of art at the museum, but just the beginning of what you can see there.

The museum boasts the largest collection of British Pre-Raphaelite art in the United States. The Wilmington area is home to the Brandywine School's style of illustration, so you'll also find a large collection of work by the founder of that style, Howard Pyle, and many of his students, including N. C. Wyeth, Maxfield Parrish, and Frank E. Schoonover. Make sure you take time to wander outside through the Copeland Sculpture Garden, where the works include Tom Otterness' 13-foot *Crying Giant*.

Check the museum calendar before you go: it offers a number of programs that allow you to get in touch with your inner artist, from date nights to try your hand at pottery, sketch night happy hours, and special family days.

2301 Kentmere Pkwy.
Wilmington, DE 19806
delart.org

TIP
Admission is free every Sunday year-round and after 4:00 p.m. on Thursdays from April to December.

SHOPPING AND FASHION

CATCH A STORY
AT BROWSEABOUT BOOKS

Browseabout Books is more than just a business that sells books. It's also a gathering place: for book clubs, for for VIPs like television host Hoda Kotb, for youngsters of all ages at the shop's regular storytimes, and for fans at book signings and readings by acclaimed authors. A mainstay of Rehoboth Beach's main thoroughfare, Browseabout has transformed itself and expanded over the decades to add local gifts, toys, cards, and coffee while still keeping its books front and center. It's open year-round even when other stores at the beach are shuttered, so even on a chilly winter day it's a place to pop in and shop. It carries national best sellers, comic books, a good supply of used beach-read paperbacks, and an excellent selection of children's and teens' books to whet the appetites of younger readers.

133 Rehoboth Ave.
Rehoboth Beach, DE 19971
(302) 226-2665
browseaboutbooks.com

TIP

An always-changing highlight is the section of staff picks near the front of the store, including both fiction and nonfiction recommended by Browseabout's well-read experts.

TAKE ADVANTAGE
OF TAX-FREE SHOPPING
AT CHRISTIANA MALL

A day at Christiana Mall might have been what Delaware's government officials had in mind more than a decade ago when they installed signs at the state line declaring the First State "Home of Tax-Free Shopping." The signs have since been replaced, but the mall remains a regional shopping destination where, as advertised, you'll pay exactly what the price tag says—and not a penny more.

Renovated in 2014, the mall boasts 1,267,241 square feet of retail space and nearly 180 retailers that will appeal to all shopping tastes. Along with anchor stores Nordstrom, Macy's, J. C. Penney, and Target, the mall features speciality retailers and brands, including Apple, Anthropologie, Coach, Sephora, H&M, LEGO, and Barnes & Noble. Along with the standard mall food court, dining options include Brio, the Cheesecake Factory, California Pizza Kitchen, and Panera. Outdoor enthusiasts can visit the freestanding Cabela's located on the mall perimeter, while cinephiles can take in a movie at the 17-screen Cinemark theatre.

Save time to visit the adjacent Christiana Fashion Center, an outdoor shopping center that is home to the First State's only REI, Nordstrom Rack, and Shake Shack. You can also take a break from shopping at Main Event, a 50,000-square-foot entertainment center with 22 bowling lanes, laser tag, video games, and a restaurant.

TIP

The crowds inside the tax-free Apple
store can be intimidating even on weekdays.
Arrive early and be prepared for a wait.

132 N. Christiana Mall
Newark, DE 19702
(302) 731-9815
christianamall.com

DRESS FOR LESS
AT TANGER OUTLETS

Had enough sand and surf? Trade in the beach for bargain shopping with a visit to Rehoboth's Tanger Outlets. Spread out over three locations along Coastal Highway (Delaware Route 1), the outlets boast 557,353 square feet of tax-free retail space. Tenants include such high-end designer brands as Coach, Dooney & Bourke, and Helly Hansen, and more affordable labels like J. Crew, American Eagle, and Gap.

Traffic can be a hassle during the busy summer season, but there are several options for avoiding the gridlock. A shuttle from the Lewes Ferry Terminal runs from June 1 to September 30, stopping at all three outlet locations before returning to the terminal. DART, the statewide bus system, serves two park and ride lots along Route 1 in Lewes and Rehoboth Beach connecting the outlets with a number of area attractions and hotels.

Tanger Surfside
35000 Midway Outlet Dr.
Rehoboth Beach, DE 19971

Tanger Bayside
36720 Bayside Outlet Dr.

Tanger Seaside
36740 Seaside Outlet Dr.

(302) 226-9223
tangeroutlet.com/rehoboth

GET YOUR HAUL
OF ANTIQUE ITEMS
AND VINTAGE ARTIFACTS

If you're into antiquing, then a drive through southern Delaware will make you feel that you've hit the jackpot. Whether you're looking for glassware, old toys, furniture, clothing, signs, magazines, or jewelry, you'll find what you're seeking—and enjoy the fun of the hunt. These shops range from highway haunts to downtown stroll-ins, single-owner stores to multi-vendor operations, and you never quite know what you're going to find tucked away on a shelf in the basement of an old converted house. But if you're seeking out a 1960s Boy Scout Handbook, a 1930s postcard of Wooster, Ohio, or a classic grandfather clock, you just might stumble across it here.

Antique Alley
225 Main St.
Millsboro, DE 19966
(302) 934-9841

Bean's Attic
8303 Dupont Blvd.
Lincoln, DE 19960
(302) 422-5195

Antique Alley of Bridgeville
18208 Sussex Hwy. (Route 13)
Bridgeville, DE 19933
(302) 337-3137

The Mercantile at Milton
109 Union St.
Milton, DE 19968
(302) 664-1840

VISIT THE MOST
ECLECTIC GROCERY STORE ANYWHERE

You know something's different walking into Byler's stores in Dover and Harrington. For one, there are often horse-drawn buggies at a hitching post in the parking lot, hailing from the region's vibrant Amish community. And two, there's a hand-scooped ice cream stand greeting everyone who comes through the doors. Byler's is a grocery store with a discount twist. At the center of the store are bargain grocery goods, such as canned items, cereals, paper products, and snacks, stacked up without the benefit of shelves. But the real gems are found in the bulk food and bakery areas—30 types of flour, countless spices, pastas, grains, off-the-wall sugary snacks, and specialty baking ingredients galore. You want a large box of honey-roasted sesame sticks, a huge bag of giant mushroom popcorn kernels, or in-house pies, breads, and rolls? You'll find them at Byler's. The Dover store also features a large gift shop with home decor, kitchenware, and cookbooks as well as a stove outlet offering grills, fireplaces, pellet stoves, and much more.

Byler's in West Dover
1368 Rose Valley School Rd.
Dover, DE 19904
(302) 674-1689, bylers.com

Byler's in Harrington
17104 S. Dupont Hwy.
Harrington, DE 19952
(302) 398-0398, bylers.com

TIP
Both stores are closed Sunday, so get your shopping done before then!

EXPLORE THE ART OF STAINED GLASS
AT D & D

Stained glass isn't found only in church windows, but is an art form that's quite easy to get into. Walking into the small storefront of D & D Stained Glass in downtown Millsboro is a dazzling experience—quite literally, with light reflecting off a huge array of premade items and glass sheets. You can walk out with a gift ranging from plates to ornaments and windows to candy dishes, or if you're already into making creations of your own, you can buy sheets of glass in an astounding array of colors as well as basic tools and other supplies. Artist Debra Doucette offers classes to teach basic stained glass, mosaics, and fusing, and the shop creates and installs custom-designed panels for shaped windows.

205 Washington St.
Millsboro, DE 19966
(302) 934-6220
ddstainedglass.com

GET IN TOUCH
WITH YOUR INNER COLLEGE STUDENT IN DOWNTOWN NEWARK

Home of the University of Delaware, Newark (pronounced new-ark) has all the hallmarks of the quintessential college town on its aptly named Main Street: eclectic shops, plenty of coffee spots, and a mix of independent restaurants.

Stop into Newark Deli and Bagels for a breakfast sandwich, or grab coffee and a snack from BrewHaHa and munch while you browse. Buy Blue Hens gear and check out the mix of kitchen gadgets, school supplies, and party decorations at National 5 and 10, which has been owned by the same family since 1911. Pick up unique gifts at Bloom or indulge your inner nerd at The Days of Knights, which specializes in games and collectables.

Part of the UD campus intersects with the downtown area. On warm days, join the students on the lawn. Or wander up to the Newark Shopping Center and explore the unique food finds at Newark Natural Foods, a grocery co-op and cafe.

TIP
If you park in a city lot and spend money at a local business, make sure to ask about parking validation, which would give you a discount on the rate.

Newark Deli and Bagels
36 E. Main St.
Newark, DE 19711
(302) 266-7150, newarkdeliandbagels.com

BrewHaHa
45 E. Main St. (Second Floor)
Newark, DE 19711
(302) 369-2600, brewhaha.com

National 5 and 10
66 E. Main St.
Newark, DE 19711
(302) 368-1646, national5and10.com

Bloom
165 E. Main St. #2
Newark, DE 19711
(302) 454-7266, bloomfolly.com

The Days of Knights
173 E. Main St.
Newark, DE 19711
(302) 366-0963, daysofknights.com
daysofknights@comcast.net

Newark Natural Foods
209 Newark Shopping Center
Newark, DE 19711
(302) 368-5894, newark.coop
info@newarknaturalfoods.com

DO SOME SHOPPING
WHILE TAKING A HISTORIC HOME TOUR IN DOWNTOWN LEWES

The beach in Lewes is about a mile and a half from the main downtown area, but you're missing out if all you do is drive through.

If you visit between April and October, check out the Zwaanendael Museum, named after the colony established by the Dutch in 1631 and dedicated to the city's maritime, military, and social history. Then wander over to Shipcarpenter Street, where you can see a group of nine historic buildings maintained by the Lewes Historical Society.

On the way (it's about a 10-minute walk if you don't stop), check out some of the local shops and restaurants. Pick up toys or clothing for your favorite young person at Kids' Ketch, check out the well-curated stock of rare and used books at Biblion, and get a snack at the Wonka-esque Edie Bees candy store or King's ice cream. Sit-down options include brunches with a twist at Nectar or Honey's Farm Fresh Gourmet, seafood at Striper Bites, or Mexican at Agave. You'll head home pleasantly full, carrying shopping bags of unique finds and with a boosted historical IQ.

TIP

If you visit during the off-season, make sure you check the hours of the restaurants, shops, and attractions: some close for the winter, and others reduce their hours.

Zwaanendael Museum
102 Kings Hwy.
Lewes, DE 19958
(302) 645-1148
history.delaware.gov/zm_main/

Lewes Historical Society Shipcarpenter Campus
110 Shipcarpenter St.
Lewes, DE 19958
(302) 645-7670
info@historiclewes.org
historiclewes.org

Kids' Ketch
132 Second St.
Lewes, DE 19958
(302) 645-8448
kidsketch.com

Biblion
205 Second St.
Lewes, DE 19958
(302) 644-2210
biblionbooks.com

Edie Bees
115 Second St.
Lewes, DE 19958
(302) 645-2337

King's Homemade Ice Cream
201 Second St.
Lewes, DE 19958
(302) 645-9425
kingshomemadeicecream.com

Nectar Cafe & Juice Bar
111 Neils Alley
Lewes, DE 19958
(302) 645-5842
cafenectar.com

Honey's Farm Fresh Gourmet
329 Savannah Rd. #1438
Lewes, DE 19958
(302) 644-8400
facebook.com/honeysfarmfresh

Striper Bites
107 E. Savannah Rd.
Lewes, DE 19958
(302) 645-4657
striperbites.com

Agave
137 Second St.
Lewes, DE 19958
(302) 645-1232
agavelewes.com

SUGGESTED
ITINERARIES

IN & AROUND WILMINGTON

View Famous Art and Make Some of Your Own at the
Delaware Art Museum, 149

See Art on the Cutting Edge at the Contemporary, 123

Eat Sausage Made By "The King" at Maiale Deli & Salumeria, 18

Try "Unapologetically Vegan" Food at Drop Squad Kitchen, 29

Watch the Seasons Change at Brandywine Park, 106

YOUNG FAMILIES

Let Your Kids Take the Lead at the Delaware Children's Museum, 58

Travel on a Replica of a 1600s-Era Sailing Ship, 124

Catch a Story at Browseabout Books, 152

Get a Farm-Fresh Taste of Delaware Ice Cream, 2

Take a Relaxing Ride on an Old-Fashioned Railway, 44

Feel like Royalty by Building a Sandcastle on the Beach, 108

WITH TEENS

Sample 100 Different Flavors of Ice Cream at the Beach, 28

Watch Sports. Lots of Them, 98

Set Foot on a Civil War Island Prison, 116

Don't Miss the Milk Shakes or the Burgers, at the Charcoal Pit, 15

Get Your Climb On in the Trees or at the Gym, 72

Paddle Up to a Lighthouse in the Delaware Bay, 77

FREE

DATE NIGHT

ON THE FARM

ACTIVITIES
BY SEASON

SPRING

Hike or Bike the Trails, No Elevation Here, 76

Tour Historic Aircraft on an Air Force Base, 142

Meet Your Local Farmers at Community Farmers Markets, 17

Learn about Old-Time Heroes at a Historic Lifesaving Station, 120

See Birds from All Over the World at Stunning Wildlife Refuges, 112

SUMMER

Travel on a Replica of a 1600s-Era Sailing Ship, 124

Get a Farm-Fresh Taste of Delaware Ice Cream, 2

Sample 100 Different Flavors of Ice Cream at the Beach, 28

Enjoy the Quintessential Beach Treat of Dolle's Candyland, 8

Rent a Bike for Relaxing Resort Cycling, 78

Get Your Outdoors Fix Camping at a Prime Sweet Spot, 100

Skimboard with the Pros at Dewey Beach, 102

FALL

Watch Sports. Lots of Them., 98

Peer inside the Workings of a Historic Mill, 121

Visit the Animals at Delaware's Lone Zoo, 56

Get a Bird's-Eye View in Rockford Park, 145

Salute the Greatest Generation with a Visit to Fort Miles, 139

Travel on a Replica of a 1600s-Era Sailing Ship, 124

WINTER

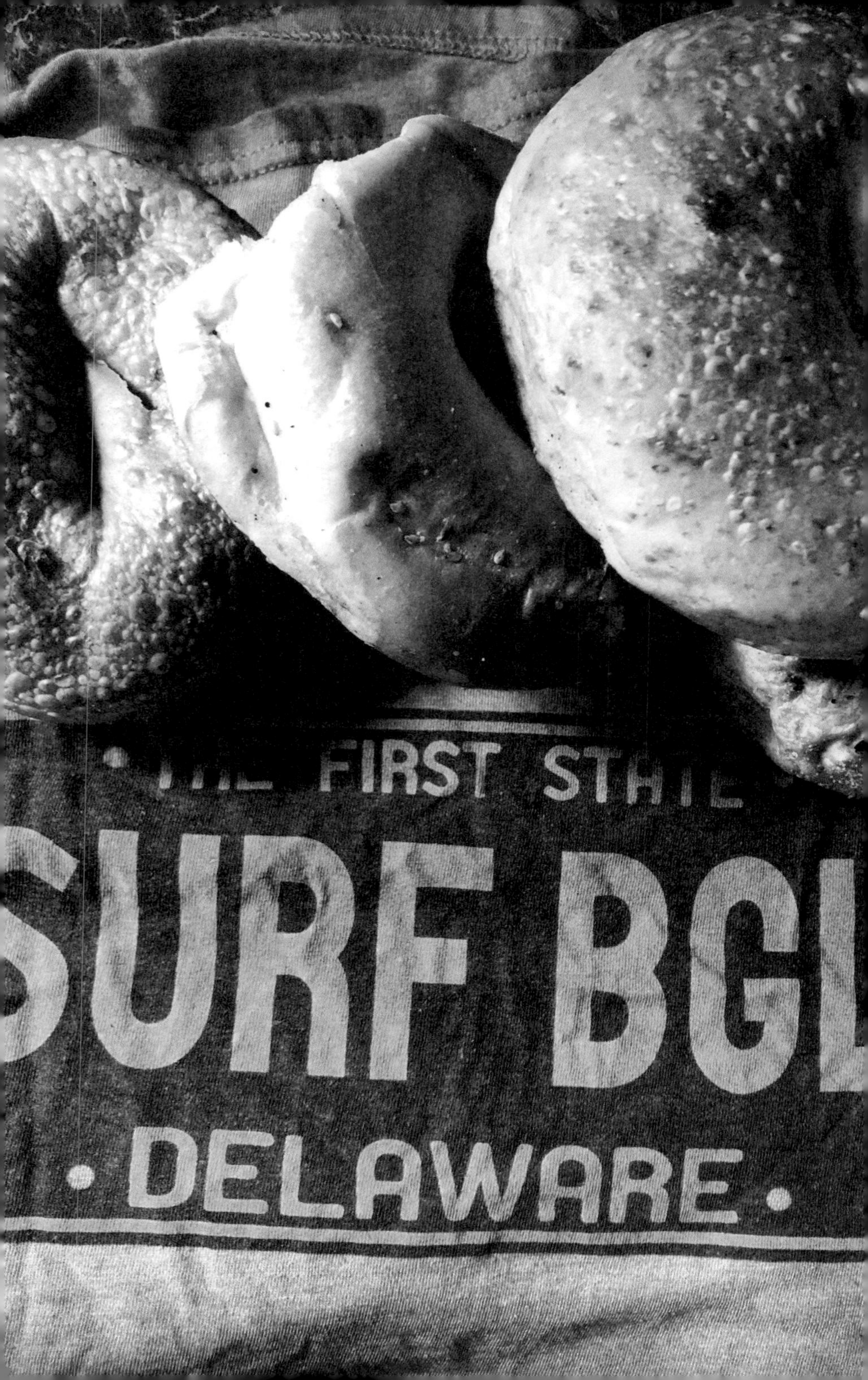
THE FIRST STATE
SURF BGL
DELAWARE

INDEX

Richard Wagner's Visit to Rossini
and
An Evening at Rossini's in Beau-Sejour

Richard Wagner's Visit to Rossini (*Paris 1860*)
AND
An Evening at Rossini's in Beau-Sejour (*Passy*) 18ʒ8
by Edmond Michotte

translated from the French and annotated,
with an introduction and appendix, by

HERBERT WEINSTOCK

The University of Chicago Press
Chicago and London

Designed and illustrated by Warren Chappell

Library of Congress Catalog Card Number: 68-16706
The University of Chicago Press, Chicago 60637
The University of Chicago Press, Ltd., London W.C.1
© 1968 by The University of Chicago
All rights reserved. Published 1968
Phoenix edition 1982
Printed in the United States of America

89 88 87 86 85 84 83 82   2 3 4 5 6

ISBN: 0-226-52442-6 (cloth)
0-226-52443-4 (paper)

Preface

EDMOND MICHOTTE (1830–1914), a wealthy Belgian amateur composer-pianist, achieved some notoriety by his propagandizing for (and performances on) the Mattauphone, a set of thirty-eight graduated musical glasses in a rectangular box which were tuned by increasing or decreasing the amount of water in each of them. Invented in about 1855 by Joseph Mattau of Brussels, the Mattauphone was made to sound by rubbing wet fingers around the rims of its constituent glasses. Michotte, however, was not any sort of eccentric: he was for many years President of the Administrative Council of the Conservatoire Royal de Musique at Brussels, to which he gave his large, important collection of Rossiniana, which notably includes many of Isabella Colbran Rossini's opera scores, the collection of first-printed librettos of Rossini's operas formed by the composer's father, and various memorabilia. In his Brussels palace, Michotte gave the first (private concert) performance in Belgium of Boito's *Mefistofele*. Some time after 1893, he published privately a thirty-one-page booklet entitled *Souvenirs: Une Soirée chez Rossini à Beau-Séjour (Passy) 1858*, a wonderfully vivid account of an evening at the Villa Rossini during which the sixty-six-year-old composer set forth the principles and practice of *bel canto* as that "lost art" had been understood in his youth.

More importantly, Michotte issued at Paris in 1906 (but had printed at Brussels) a fifty-three-page booklet, the cover of which is reproduced here. The present book is a textually complete translation of Michotte's two booklets, to which an Appendix adds translations of brief accounts by Eduard Hanslick (1860 and 1867) and by Emil Naumann (1867) of calls on Rossini.

Doubt naturally has been expressed about the reliability of Michotte's detailed reproduction of the conversation between Rossini and Wagner. Ernest Newman began by referring slightingly to Michotte (*The Life of Richard Wagner*, 4 vol. [New York, 1933–41], III, 12):

> It was in March 1860 that Wagner and Rossini met for the only time in their lives. In 1906 one E. * Michotte published a brochure in which he

---

* Surely Newman could have ascertained Michotte's given name and identity?

claimed [italics mine] that he had been a member of the small circle of literary men who gathered round Wagner in Paris in 1860, that it was he who took Wagner to Rossini's house and introduced him, and that his brochure is based on notes made at the time of the conversation between the two. Wagner nowhere makes any mention of Michotte: perhaps he had forgotten his existence when he came to write *Mein Leben.*

Then, having conceded some credibility to Michotte's account because it agrees "in essence" with the accounts given by Wagner (a notoriously bad witness) in *Mein Leben* and the "Erinnerungen an Rossini" that he wrote for the Augsburg *Allgemeine Zeitung* (December 17, 1868) right after Rossini's death, Newman says, without specifications: "His little book contains many errors on points of fact; * but biographers and historians will hardly expect from any man a minutely accurate recollection of a conversation of nearly half a century before." (Michotte had not claimed to recollect the conversation; he stated that he had preserved the notes that he had taken of it in 1860.)

---

* Michotte erred in describing *Der Ring des Nibelungen* as then (1860) "almost finished"; in saying that in 1860 Wagner "just had finished" the scenario of *Die Meistersinger von Nürnberg;* and perhaps in calling Gustave Doré a "close friend" of Wagner—though the two men were more than merely acquainted. But it seems tendentious to call three errors "many."

Finally, Newman, convinced of Michotte's reliability for reasons that he does not advance, swings around completely: "All in all, however, when full allowance has been made for Michotte's mistakes and embroideries, there seems little reason to doubt that he was present at the interview, and that the talk was substantially as he represents it to have been." The present writer, having become familiar, during years of research into the life of Rossini, with Michotte's dignified and completely honorable character, finds no doubt possible that the Belgian was a reliable, truth-telling witness.

Ernest Newman was much more generous to Rossini than to "one E. Michotte":

> Rossini can certainly be acquitted of any ill-will towards Wagner: he was neither fool enough to be blind to the fact that there must be something in the man who could win such admiration from men of the quality of Liszt, Bülow and many others, nor base enough to see merely an occasion for witticisms in the spectacle of an idealist fighting for his very life against journalistic gangsters the real character of whom no one knew better than Rossini himself.

The fact is that thanks to Michotte's meticulous note taking and his preservation of the notes for more than forty-five years, we have an almost stenographic report of a conversation between

E. MICHOTTE

SOUVENIRS PERSONNELS

LA VISITE

DE

R. WAGNER A ROSSINI

(PARIS 1860)

DETAILS INEDITS

ET

COMMENTAIRES

(AVEC PORTRAITS)

1906

Paris G. Rossini 1860

THE PORTRAITS of Wagner and Rossini included herein are enlargements of photograph cards (that of Wagner by P. Petit, that of Rossini by Numa Blanc) which were given to me by the two masters precisely in 1860, at the time when their interview took place. Wagner, exhausted by work, was then very thin.

Rossini and Wagner in Paris in 1860, one year
before the notorious production of *Tannhäuser* at
the Opéra, four years before Rossini's composition
of the *Petite Messe solennelle*. Michotte, who ap-
preciated and befriended Wagner and was on
terms of the closest friendship with Rossini during
the last dozen years of the Italian composer's life,
cannot, of course, have written down verbatim everything that the two men said while they were
saying it. The booklet that he published in 1906
nonetheless performs the near miracle of bringing
us, across the decay and destruction of more than a
century, an approximate transcript of their conversation, thus providing not only an exposition by
Wagner of his theories about the music drama but
also firsthand reports by Rossini—an acute ob-
server—of meetings with Beethoven, Weber, and
Mendelssohn. *La Visite de R. Wagner à Rossini
(Paris 1860)* is a unique and invaluable document.

Une *Soirée chez Rossini à Beau-Sejour
(Passy) 1858*, less of a mother lode, is scarcely less
interesting, for it brings us Rossini's own ideas
about *bel canto*, singing in general, and many of the
great singers of the first half of the nineteenth century. In an Appendix, I have subjoined to the two
Michotte texts translations of shorter conversations
with Rossini by Eduard Hanslick and Emil Naumann, both interesting in themselves and both

throwing further light on Rossini's attitudes toward Wagner.

With heavy-handed irony, chance brought death to the eighty-four-year-old Michotte in the Séminaire Léon XIII at Louvain, where he had taken refuge during the burning of his chateau by German soldiers: the date was August 31, 1914.

HERBERT WEINSTOCK

NOTE TO THE READER: *Numbered footnotes are Michotte's; other footnotes and any words in square brackets have been inserted by me. Points of suspension are in Michotte's published texts: I have deleted nothing in the translation.* H. W.

CONTENTS

xi

(MICHOTTE'S DEDICATORY LETTER)

TO

*A. Gevaert**

M<small>Y GOOD FRIEND</small>, you will recall the concert that R. Wagner organized at the Théâtre-Italien [Salle Ventadour] in Paris (January 25, 1860), the concert in which, under his own direction, he permitted us to hear for the first time (I have the program here at hand):

> The Overture to *Der fliegende Holländer*
> The Overture and March with chorus from
>   *Tannhäuser*

---

* François-Auguste Gevaert (1828–1908), Belgian musicologist and composer.

The Prelude and Wedding Celebration from
  Lohengrin
The Prelude to *Tristan und Isolde* *

In the musical world of that time, it was the sort of event to arouse Parisian curiosity to a fever because of the violent polemics that had been provoked in the public press by the appearance of Wagner's revolutionary writings concerning his very daring ideas about reforming the music drama.

People went in crowds to see the man, to hear his works.

You will remember the effervescence of that disturbed audience; the very strange atmosphere in the hall, where a number of partisan fanatics did not restrain themselves at all from manifesting their hostile feelings overtly; where others—poseurs as much as ignoramuses—thought it good form to attract attention to themselves by raillery and persiflage; while some listeners, truly impressed, nonetheless did not dare to express their opinion except as hedged about with multiple re-

---

* The audience burst into applause after the seventeenth measure of the *Tannhäuser* March, but was baffled by the *Tristan* Prelude, of which Wagner had written to Mathilde Wesendonk that it was "so incomprehensibly *new* to the musicians that I had to lead them from note to note as though prospecting for precious stones in a mine."

strictions intended to dilute the too-laudatory burden of their approval.

A very agitated group had gathered in the
lobby during the interruption that preceded the
second part of the program. A circle was formed
around Halévy, Ambroise Thomas, Auber, Clapisson, etc.*

The *Tannhäuser* Overture was under discussion . . .

You arrived.

"And you, Gevaert," Jouvin ** exclaimed,
"what do you have to say about that farce of an
overture, toward which one would be showing excessive politeness if one did not swallow it as
though it were the overture to a . . . farce?"

"What I'd say," you replied, "is that I wish
that I had done it as a way of taking the shortest
road to posterity."

"Ah! You make good jokes," Jouvin retorted.

---

* Jacques-François-Fromental-Élie Halévy (1799–1862),
operatic composer (*La Juive*, etc.) and pedagogue; father-
in-law of Bizet. Ambroise Thomas (1811–1896), operatic
composer (*Hamlet, Mignon,* etc.) and pedagogue. Daniel-
François-Esprit Auber (1782–1871), composer of operas
(*Fra Diavolo, La Muette de Portici,* etc.) and operettas (*Le
Cheval de bronze, Les Diamants de la couronne,* etc.). Antoine-Louis Clapisson (1808–1866), operatic composer (*La
Perruche,* etc.) and violinist.
** Benoît-Jean-Baptiste Jouvin (1820–18??), musical journalist and biographer.

Then he added (in the manner of a *boulevardier*): "You know, *mon p'tit*, that doesn't take me in!"

And now, behold—that overture has taken the road to posterity. As your friend, I regret only that it was not you who composed it.

The above is in relation to the account to follow—*Wagner's Visit to Rossini*—an account that at first I had no intention of making public.

You know about it: the notes that I have preserved from my long relationship with Rossini —and in which I again find all the details of that interview with Wagner—in fact, I always have thought of them as a record of intimate confidences that up to now I never have dreamed of divulging outside a restricted circle of friends. Among those friends, it is true, some former intimates of the entourage of the composer of *Il Barbiere* [*di Siviglia*] who still survive often have urged me to put into print some extracts from these memories.

A similar desire was expressed to me last year when, at one of the Wagner family's receptions at Bayreuth, the course of the conversation having directed attention to the Master's visit to Rossini in 1860, I found myself able to furnish the most precise circumstantial account of the nature of that interview, at which I was present.

Taking into consideration those instances and

still others that occurred later, I yielded, and that is how it now happens that I exhume a document—buried for forty-six years in my boxes—the contents of which I dare to believe perhaps still offer a certain contemporary interest despite their retrospective nature.

Read this, my dear Gevaert, and let yourself be carried back to the time of our good years of youth in Paris—when, like me, you knew these two men of genius, later immortalized, whose physiognomies I shall re-trace and whose words I shall restate.

To you, then, the homage of these souvenirs.

Your affectionate,

E. Michotte

Brussels, April 15, 1906

Richard Wagner's Visit to Rossini

to Rossini

(Paris 1860)

[PARIS 1860]

VERY DIVERSE REPORTS used to be current about the visit that Wagner made to Rossini at the time (March, 1860) when the German Master was staying in Paris in the hope of staging his opera *Tannhäuser* there. With the help of imagination, that meeting was interpreted in the most fantastic way by the press and the public.

Wagner himself commented upon it much later in an article that he published in a Leipzig journal [1] on the occasion of Rossini's death. He did

---

[1] *Errinnerungen* [*sic*] *an Rossini* (1868) [published, not in Leipzig, but in the Augsburg *Allgemeine Zeitung* (December 17, 1868)].

9

so very briefly, not mentioning details, which perhaps he did not recall after eight years; or to which—possibly—he did not from his point of view attribute enough significant importance to decide to place them in evidence.

That interview, however, was so essentially typical that to leave an account of it in oblivion would be regrettable.

I shall recount later on how, by a series of circumstances, I, having been present, found myself in a position to be able to reproduce in a scrupulously exact narrative the various phases of the conversation that took place between these two famous men.[2]

---

[2] All the nonsense then invented on this subject—around which a legend was formed which survives even to this day—finally coalesced to claim:

That at first Rossini energetically refused to see Wagner . . .

That, being unable to evade the meeting any longer, he received him very rudely and showed special aggressiveness toward him . . .

That Wagner, very uneasy—pale as a corpse!—stammered forth many full excuses, repented with regard to his writings . . . etc. . . . .

As many absurdities as fables.

I assert that at the time of the meeting no reporter would have had any way of knowing the smallest details of an essentially private conversation that took place unexpectedly during a courtesy call about which neither Rossini nor Wagner had any wish to satisfy public curiosity.

Also, it is to form a wrong notion of the characters of

But, at the outset, a few words to determine the positions that Rossini and Wagner occupied at that time in Paris.

It was during the winter of 1860 [March, 1860]. Wagner was living at No. 16, rue Newton (near the Barrière de l'Étoile), in a small house (later destroyed) which he had furnished mostly with his own furniture, brought from Zurich, where it had graced a residence that he had called the Azyl [*sic*]. Thence, in 1859, he had set out for France. Accustomed to those furnishings, which reminded him of a milieu that he had left regretfully, he wanted to be surrounded by various objects because constant sight of them would evoke still-vibrant memories of that wholly charming woman, that Mathilde Wesendonck for whom, during years of proximity at Zurich, he had conceived the enthusiasm about which one knows; that woman who exercised so much influence upon the direction of his genius.

---

these two great spirits to believe one of them—known for his urbanity—capable of attacking a visitor whom he had admitted to his home; and the other—who already had given more than enough proof of his indomitable courage—disposed to humble himself or stand for the least attack that would hurt his dignity.

A simple appeal to good sense suffices to destroy such assertions forever.

In that peaceful house he lived very modestly. Being near the Bois de Boulogne, he went out only to take a daily walk accompanied by a very lively dog that he loved to watch as it leaped about him. He spent the rest of the day collaborating uninterruptedly with Edmond Roche on the French translation of *Tannhäuser*.* In the intervals, he devoted himself to the tetralogy [*Der Ring des Nibelungen*], putting the final touches on the orchestration of that gigantic work, then already almost finished.**

His first wife *** lived with him and took care of the household. She was a person of bourgeois aspect, very simple, who effaced herself as much as she could.

Evenings, and particularly on Wednesdays, he received some few friends. They were about a

---

* The completed French translation of the *Tannhäuser* libretto was credited to three men: Roche, Richard Lindau, and "Charles Nuitter" (Charles-Louis-Étienne Truinet).

** In 1860, *Der Ring des Nibelungen* was far from being "almost finished": there remained to be completed the composition of *Siegfried* from the middle of Act III, the orchestration of that opera, and the composition and orchestration of *Götterdämmerung*.

*** Minna Planer (1809–1866), a minor actress, had become Wagner's wife in 1836. After a tempestuous married life that included more than one temporary separation, Wagner saw her for the last time in Dresden in November, 1862; she died there in January, 1866.

dozen, I believe, of those by whom he was not misjudged at that time and who went to seek him out in his solitude. I shall mention: Gasperini, Ed. Roche, Villot, Hans von Bülow, Champfleury, G. Doré, Lacombe, Stephen Heller, Émille Olivier [*sic*] and his young wife (Liszt's daughter) *
. . . I was fortunate in being one of those habitués, which brought me the privilege of frequent friendly contacts with Wagner, which were consolidated later on.

Wagner, who had no connections in Paris and did not seek any, was happy to have this entourage of a few faithful friends. When the bell rang to announce an arrival, one could see with what speed

---

* Agénor de Gasperini (1825?–1868), musical dilettante and writer, author of *La Nouvelle Allemagne musicale: Richard Wagner* (Paris, 1866). Edmond Roche (1828–1861), poet and musician, principal translator of the *Tannhäuser* libretto into French. Frédéric Villot, *conservateur des musées impériales,* to whom the French translations of Wagner's librettos were dedicated. Hans von Bülow (1830–1894), pianist, conductor, writer, first husband of Liszt's daughter Cosima, later Wagner's second wife. Champfleury (pseudonym of Jules Husson, also called Fleury, 1821–1889), painter, sculptor, and writer; his brochure on Wagner (1860) was republished in his *Grandes Figures d'hier et d'aujourd'hui* (1861). Gustave Doré (1833–1883), painter and engraver, close friend of Rossini and admiring acquaintance of Wagner. Louis (Brouillon) Lacombe (1818–1884), composer and pianist. Stephen Heller (1813–1888), Hungarian Jewish pianist and composer. Émile Ollivier (1825–1913), politician and cabinet minister, married Liszt's daughter Blandine.

the Master, knowing that it was one of us, rushed, alert and joyful, to greet a friend.

From that moment on, he devoted himself exuberantly to abandoned chatter. Always unforeseeable, he soon charmed us by judgments marked by great loftiness of thought on subject in esthetics, history, philosophy . . . Then there were humorous sallies of astounding verve, at times even approaching prankishness.

He expressed himself readily in French; but when ideas boiled up in his mind, the impatience that he felt while trying to find the right word suggested to him word associations which were sometimes of a very original nature.

The interest of these reunions grew even greater when Hans von Bülow was one of the visitors. Then Wagner, never having to be begged, was pleased to allow us to hear—with the great pianist accompanying—not only fragments of *Tannhäuser* (with the French text), but also parts of *Tristan*, the orchestration of which was complete. A stupefying thing—Hans von Bülow sight-read at the piano the polyphonic pages of a score in which the writing is very complex. What can one say abut that intense interpretation with which the Master initiated us into the real significance, the profound character of his thought just as

he had conceived it? What fire! what animation! what exuberance of declamation! As for his voice—not always true!! for example—*the decomposed voice of a composer*, as he jokingly said—and of a sort, he added, to put to flight all mastersingers except those of Nuremberg! An allusion to *Die Meistersinger*, the scenario of which he just had completed.*

That, then was the unknown life of Wagner in Paris. Despite his dislike of paying calls, he nevertheless had been unable to dispense with the common formalities with regard to some personages

---

* Wagner had written a preliminary sketch of the *Meistersinger* at Marienbad in 1845. He did not redraft it until 1861—or complete the libretto until late January, 1862. The score was finished only in 1867.

of the musical world. He saw Auber, Halévy, Ambroise Thomas, etc. . . . He knew Gounod.[3]

---

[3] It was after those calls that, one evening among intimates, Wagner gave us his impressions of these composers. Here is a résumé:

"Halévy's operas, façade music! . . . Would you believe that I admired them sincerely in my early youth? As one is at that naïve age, I was a bit of a ninny then. The man, whom I just saw, seemed to me cold, pretentious, not very sympathetic.

"Auber—he makes music adequate to his personality, which is fundamentally Parisian, intellectual, full of good breeding, and . . . very flirtatious, as one knows. All of that is reflected in his scores. I love him as a man and esteem him highly as a musician.

"Rossini—it's true that I haven't seen him yet, but he is caricatured as a great epicurean, stuffed not with music—of which he was emptied long ago—but with mortadella! [By 1860, it was thirty-one years since Rossini had completed *Guillaume Tell*, his last opera, eighteen years since the *Stabat Mater*.]

"Gounod—an inflamed artist, in a perpetual swoon. An irresistible charmer in conversation. An affected melodist, he lacks both depth and breadth; at most, he grazes those two qualities; but always without being able to take hold of them."

Champfleury risked answering: "One should not, however, underrate the fact that in such melodious roles as Faust and Marguerite, and above all in the Garden Scene, Gounod has introduced an expressive note not previously known in French operatic music."

At the name of Faust, Wagner jumped.

"Ah, get on with you!" he exclaimed; "I've seen that theatrical parody of our German *Faust*.

"Faust and his crony Méphisto absolutely made upon me

As for Rossini, whom he had not yet met, he was in a dilemma. Knowing that I was very intimately linked to the Italian Master, he much wanted to involve me in his hesitations. Here is what motivated them: some Parisian journals that pursued Wagner and his *music of the future* relentlessly with their sarcasms, also gave themselves the malicious pleasure of spreading among the public quantities of anecdotes cut from whole cloth and often very disagreeable about the composer of *Tannhäuser*. Wanting to lend these little histories the semblance of truth, they never hesitated a bit to

---

the effect of two ridiculous Latin Quarter students trailing a girl student.

"As for the music, it's all surface sentimentality—on a level with leather . . . kidskin . . . like gloves—with rice powder, what's more, notably in that insipid Jewel Song: '*Ah! je ris* [here a pun on *riz:* rice] *de me voire si belle en ce miroir.*' "

(Wagner hummed the first measures, then added):

"That aria, look at it, in fact, the pivot of the piece; it sums up the whole psychological gamut of that ridiculous canvas.

"O Goethe!

"For Gounod, who has a real talent, but whose temperament lacks the scope for dealing with tragic subjects, I hope that he will be discerning enough in the future to choose his librettos better! In the demi-character style, he undoubtedly would be successful."

The judgment was severe; but could anything different have been sincere from the man who had just completed *Tristan und Isolde*?

give prominence to the names of well-known people, whom they saddled with the paternity of their tittle-tattle. Rossini above all, to whom witticisms (of a taste as dubious as they were apocryphal) were attributed much too often, was cut out by

nature to be monopolized—as an always well-stocked source—by these dispensers of gossip.

It was asserted that at one of the weekly dinners at which the composer of *Il Barbiere* assembled some noted guests, at the mention of *Turbot à l'allemande* on the menu, the servants placed before the guests a very appetizing sauce, of which each then took his portion. Then nothing else was served. What did not come was the turbot. Perplexed, the guests asked one another: what does one do with this sauce? Then Rossini, mischievously enjoying their embarrassment and himself gulping down the same sauce: "And so," he exclaimed, "you still are waiting for something? Enjoy this sauce; believe me, it's excellent. As for the turbot—alas! the principal dish . . . It is just . . . at the last moment the fishman forgot to bring it; don't be surprised. Isn't it the same with the music of Wagner? . . . Good sauce, but no turbot! . . . no melody."

It was also said that, another time, a visitor entered Rossini's study and surprised the Maestro, all attention, turning the pages of an enormous score . . . that of *Tannhäuser*. After further efforts, he stopped: "At last, that isn't bad!"—and he sighed. "For half an hour I've been searching . . . now I'm beginning to understand some of it!"—The score was upside down and backward! And behold, at exactly that moment, a loud fracas was heard from the next room. "Oh! oh! what's this?" Rossini went on, "that polyphony: *Corpo di Dio!* but it strongly resembles the Venusberg orchestra." Whereupon the door was opened brusquely and the valet entered to inform the

Maestro that the maid had dropped a whole platter of cutlery!

Impressed by these stories, which he believed to be true, Wagner understandably hesitated to present himself at Rossini's home. I took pains to reassure him. I made him understand that all those nonsensical stories were pure inventions with which a hostile press amused itself by spreading them to the public. I added that Rossini—whom, because of long intimacy and daily contacts, I was in a position to know better to the bottom of his character—had too elevated a mind to demean himself by sillinesses that did not even have the merit of being witty, and against which he himself never stopped protesting vehemently.[4]

I succeeded in undeceiving Wagner, assuring him that he could present himself at Rossini's without fear, that he would be received most cordially. That decided him. He expressed the wish that I accompany him and introduce him. The meeting was set for the morning two days later.

Nevertheless, I forewarned Rossini, who at once replied: "But that goes without saying; I'll

---

[4] In fact, Rossini just had published in the newspapers a denial on the subject of these "malicious hoaxes." He used to say that he was afraid of two things in this world: catarrhs and journalists; that the former engendered *humeurs mauvaises* [distempers] in his body, and the latter a *mauvaise humeur* [bad humor] in his mind.

receive M. Wagner with the greatest pleasure. You
know my hours; come with him when you wish."
Then he added: "Have you at least made it clear to
him that I am an utter stranger to all the stupidities
about him which have been attributed to me?"

Having sketched in, with these details, the circumstance under which Wagner then found himself in Paris, I still must complete this rapid glance
by devoting the following lines to Rossini before
bringing the two masters face to face.

He then occupied, in the building at the corner of the Chaussée d'Antin and the boulevard des
Italiens, that apartment on the first floor [first
above the street floor] well known to all Parisians.[5]

In 1856, the Maestro, who had been living in
Florence, suddenly returned to Paris—that Paris
which he had not seen since 1836.[*]

---

[5] It has been established that about a century earlier than
the composer of *Il Barbiere*—O, coincidence!—the composer
of *Le Nozze di Figaro*, Mozart, then staying in Paris, had
lodged in a building that then occupied the location on
which the large house mentioned above rises today. That
was the home of [Friedrich Melchior, Baron von] Grimm
(1778), with whom Mozart took refuge after having left the
rue du Gros-Chenet, where he had lost his mother.

[*] In fact, Rossini, having left Paris in 1836, returned there
in May, 1843 for four months of medical treatment. His final
return to Paris occurred in 1855, not 1856.

Having suffered from neurasthenia for some time, he had vainly sought help from Florentine physicians, who had not succeeded in fighting the trouble. It grew progressively worse. There was serious disquiet about the illustrious invalid's reason.

Mme [Olympe Pélissier] Rossini decided that a change of milieu was required. She considered Paris, where her husband had left behind solid friendships among numerous admirers. More even than on the help of therapeutics, she counted on the joys of returning to old friends, on the attractions of a new environment—all things of a nature, she thought, to influence beneficially her husband's enfeebled and discouraged moral state.

To conquer Rossini's resistance was not easy at first; to induce him to undertake such a journey, which he would have to make by post chaise, with frequent stops to change horses and halts at all the villages in which they would have to spend the night. For Rossini obstinately refused to travel by railroad.[6] He advanced as an excuse that to be conveyed at the will of a machine was too humiliating . . . to feel oneself transported like a package. But at bottom, by a bizarrerie of his nervous system, he was frankly afraid of the railroad.

Finally he consented. After a fifteen-day journey,* he reached Paris enfeebled and looking absolutely lamentable. The condition of his nerves, already forcefully upset by his illness, had been aggravated by the jolting and sudden turns of the journey. Upon seeing him with his face ashen, ex-

---

[6] The only trip by rail which he ever had risked had taken place during his visit to Belgium (1836), on the line from Brussels to Antwerp, so that he could admire the masterpieces of Rubens in the city where the painter had lived. "I still tremble in all my members," he said, "each time I think about it." [For Rossini's tragicomic musical reaction to that ride, see his "Un Petit Train de plaisir," from the Péchés de vieillesse, published in Quaderni Rossiniani, II, (Pesaro, 1954), 42.]

* Actually, the Rossinis left Florence on April 26, 1855, and reached Paris about May 25.

pressionless, his speech halting, his mind shadowed, his friends were consternated. In view of those symptoms, they could not conceal the fear that incurable softening of the brain was to be dreaded.

Thanks to the devotion of eminent practitioners, medical science succeeded in a few months in conquering that alarming condition; and as his body gradually became reestablished, the comfortable surroundings that his attentive friends were able to create around the Maestro finally relighted the flame of a mind that had been feared extinguished forever. Later, a cure at Kissingen completed the recovery. The signs of a disease that had seemed incurable were dissipated completely.

In Paris from then on, the composer of *Guillaume Tell* and *Il Barbiere* acquired an aura of glory and prestige which no one else in the musical domain equaled. His receptions became famous. The most renowned artists intrigued for the favor of having him near them. When his salons were opened, one saw the most illustrious people from all Parisian circles jostling one another there.

Amid that intellectual royalty, enveloped in an Olympian calm brought about by age, Rossini remained simple, good, affable, disdainful of arrogance, an enemy to all ostentation. And may I be permitted, in that regard, to make a *tabula rasa* of his very exaggerated reputation as a *jester* and his very undeserved one as a *scoffer*, which the Parisian journals of the time delighted to bestow upon him, attributing to him with incredible irresponsibility numerous retorts of more or less dubious taste which he never had imagined and that irreverent facetiousness toward others of which he was incapable.* He suffered from that bitter publicity, which often passed the boundaries of mischief and became frankly perfidious at his expense. He often complained, and then someone would reply: "You know, Maestro, one lends only to the rich." "To tell the truth," he would sigh, "I'd like better a little more *poverty* and a little less *generosity*. In the process of wanting to give to me, they overload, they obstruct me! And what gifts, good Lord!—garbage that splashes onto me even more than it hits the other! That exaperates me: *ma così va il mondo*."

In these few lines I have wanted to describe the very different positions occupied in Paris at that time by the two men who were about to meet. The one adulated like a demigod; the other lacking any prestige, even scoffed at, almost like a wrongdoer. And nonetheless, let us not forget, Wagner at the apogee of his genius—as great in his own eyes as he

---

* Here, protesting in a good cause, Michotte protested too much.

later showed himself to be to the generality—already had created the titanic work that slept there—ignored and colossal—in a corner of the modest quarters in the rue Newton: *Tristan und Isolde* entirely complete and the tetralogy of the *Nibelungen* on the point of being completed.*

As we had agreed, Wagner, keeping the rendezvous (which he had taken the superfluous care to recall to me again by letter very early that morning) came to call for me at my home. That was a few steps from Rossini's home, and we discussed him as soon as we were on the way.

When we were going up the stairs, I said to Wagner: "If Rossini is in a good mood, you will be charmed by his conversation. This will be a treat. Don't be surprised if you see me taking some notes during your interview . . ."

"For the newspapers?" Wagner asked.

"Not at all," I told him, "just for my personal souvenirs. If the Maestro were to gather the smallest notion that I could give material to the press, he would scarcely open his mouth. But then, he has full confidence in my discretion, whereas he hates any publicity at all about his private life."

---

* In fact, only part of *Siegfried* and none of *Götterdämmerung* had been composed. *Der Ring des Nibelungen* was completed only on November 21, 1874.

Assigning almost complete use of the apartment to his wife, Rossini had reserved for himself next to the dining room a corner with four windows looking onto the boulevard and consisting of a den that he never entered and a bedroom that he never left. A bed, a writing table, a secretary, and a small upright Pleyel piano made up the entire furnishing of this room, which was of extreme simplicity. There he unvaryingly received all callers, from the most modest of favor seekers to excellencies, highnesses, and crowned heads. There, also, he received Wagner.

When we were announced, the Maestro was just finishing his lunch. We waited for several minutes in the grand salon.

There Wagner's glance immediately lighted upon a portrait of Rossini in which he was represented half-length, life-size, wrapped in a long green mantle and with his head covered by a red cap—a portrait that has been reproduced in gravure and later became well known.

"That intelligent physiognomy, that ironic mouth—it was surely the composer of *Il Barbiere*," Wagner said to me. "That portrait must date from the period in which that opera was composed?"

"Four years later," I told him; "this portrait, painted by Mayer at Naples, dates from 1820."

"He was a good-looking youth, and in that land of Vesuvius, where women are easily ignited, he must have caused lots of ravages," Wagner answered, smiling.

"Who knows?" I said—"if he had had a valet as devoted to bookkeeping as Don Giovanni's Leporello, mightn't he perhaps have surpassed the number *mil e tre* set down in the notebook?" *

"Oh, how you exaggerate!" Wagner answered. "*Mil* I'll agree to, but *tre* more—that's really too many."

At this moment, the *valet de chambre* came to tell us that Rossini was awaiting us.

As soon as we entered, "Ah! *monsieur Wagner*," he said, "like a new Orpheus, you don't fear to enter this redoubtable precinct . . ." And, without giving Wagner time to reply: "I know that they have thoroughly blackened me in your mind . . ."[7]

---

* Leporello, reading to Donna Elvira from his copious notebok the number of Don Giovanni's female conquests, says that in Spain they numbered *"mil e tre"* (one thousand and three).

[7] In reporting the conversation between the two masters, I have tried to reproduce it integrally as much as possible. It is quasi-verbatim, in particular as far as Rossini is concerned, he having married as his second wife Olympe Pélissier, a *parisienne,* and being accustomed to speak French, of which he knew all the fine points, argot included. As for

"With regard to you, they load me with many quips that, what is more, nothing could justify on my part. And why do *I* suffer from this fate? I am neither Mozart nor Beethoven. Nor do I pretend to be a wise man; but I do hold to being polite and refraining from insulting a musician who, like you—for this is what I have been told—is trying to extend the limits of our art. Those great devils who take pleasure in busying themselves with me should at least grant that, though I lack other merits, I do have some common sense.

"As for slighting your music, I should have to be familiar with it first; to know it, I should have to hear it in the theater, as only in the theater, and not by the mere reading of a score, is it possible to bring equitable judgment to bear on music intended for the stage. The only composition of yours which I know is the March from *Tannhäuser*. I heard it often at Kissingen when I was taking the cure there three years ago. It made a great effect, and—I assure you sincerely—as for me, I thought it very beautiful.

"And now that—I hope—all misunderstanding between us has been dissipated, tell me how you

Wagner, less familiar with this language, he frequently multiplied circumlocutions in the attempt to express his thought precisely. I have thought it my duty at times to sum up in more literary language what he said.

are finding your stay in Paris. I know that you are in discussions about staging your opera *Tannhäuser*? . . ."

Wagner seemed impressed by that welcoming preamble, spoken in a simple tone full of great good

nature. "Allow me," he responded, "illustrious *Maître*, to thank you for these friendly words. They touch me deeply. They show me how much, in the welcome that you want to accord me, your character—which I never have doubted—displays nobility and greatness. Believe, above all, I beg you, that even if you criticize me sharply, I shall take no offense. I know that my writings are of a sort to give birth to wrong interpretations. Faced with the exposition of a huge system of new ideas, the best-intentioned judges can mistake their significance. That comes about because I am late in being

able to make a logical and complete demonstration of my tendencies by performances, as complete and nearly perfect as possible, of my operas."

ROSSINI: "That is fair: for deeds are worth more than words!"

WAGNER: "And, to begin with, all my efforts at this moment are toward getting *Tannhäuser* performed. I recently played it for Carvalho,* who was favorably impressed and seemed disposed to attempt the adventure; but nothing has been decided yet. Unhappily, the ill will that has raged against me in the press for so long threatens to take the form of a real cabal . . . It is to be feared that Carvalho may fall under its influence . . ."

At the word "cabal," ROSSINI (animatedly): "What composer," he interjected, "has not felt them, to begin with the great Gluck himself? As for me, I was not spared—far from it. On the evening of the *première* of *Il Barbiere*, when, as was customary then in Italy for *opera buffa*, I played the clavicembalo in the orchestra to accompany the recitatives, I had to protect myself from a really riotous attitude on the part of the audience. I thought that they were going to assassinate me.

"Here in Paris, where I came for the first time in 1824,** having been summoned by the direction of the Théâtre-Italien, I was greeted by the sobriquet 'Monsieur Vacarmini' [Mr. Uproar], which I still have. And it's not a thing of the past, I assure you, for me to be abused in the camp of some

---

* Léon Carvaille, called Carvalho (1825–1897), stage director of the Opéra, Paris, and husband of the noted soprano Marie Miolan-Carvalho.

** Rossini actually reached Paris for the first time in November, 1823.

musicians and press critics leagued in a common accord—an accord as perfect as it is major! *

"It was no different in Vienna when I arrived there in 1822 to mount my opera *Zelmira*. [Carl Maria von] Weber himself—who, what is more, had been fulminating against me in articles for a long time—pursued me relentlessly after the performances of my operas at the Italian court theater. . ."

WAGNER: "Weber, oh! I know he was very intolerant. He became intractable above all when it was a question of defending German art. That could be forgiven him; so that—and this is understandable—you did not have friendly relations

* A pun on the French *accord*, which means both "accord" or "harmony" and "chord."

with him during your stay in Vienna? A great genius, and so prematurely dead!"

ROSSINI: "A great genius certainly, and a true one he was; for, being creative and strong within himself, he imitated no one. In fact, I didn't meet him in Vienna; but, you see, as a result of those circumstances I saw him later in Paris, where he stopped off a few days before starting for England. Immediately after his arrival, he paid the customary calls on leading musicians—Cherubini, Hérold, Boieldieu. Not having foreseen his visit, I must admit that when I found myself unexpectedly facing that composer of genius, I felt an emotion not too unlike the one that I had felt earlier upon finding myself in the presence of Beethoven. Very pallid, breathless from having climbed my stairs (for he was already very ill), as soon as he saw me the poor fellow thought it necessary to tell me—with an embarrassment that his difficulty in finding French words increased even more—that he had been very hard on me in his critical articles on music . . . but . . . I didn't let him finish . . . 'Look,' I told him, 'let's not discuss that. To begin with,' I added, 'those articles—I've never read them; I don't know German . . . the only words of your language, which is devilish for a musician, which I was able, after heroic application, to re-member and pronounce were *ich bin zufrieden* [I am delighted].' These remarks made Weber smile, and that immediately gave him more assurance and put him at his ease.[8]

---

[8] Here, on this subject, a very amusing encounter that I shall let Rossini himself recount:

"During one of my walks in the Vienna streets, I witnessed a scuffle between two Bohemians, one of whom fell to the sidewalk after receiving a violent dagger thrust.

"Suddenly, the collecting of a huge crowd, from which I was about to escape when I was accosted by a police agent who was very agitated and said a few German words to me which I didn't understand.

"I answered him very politely: *ich bin zufrieden;* suddenly, questions, the violence of which appeared to me to be going *crescendo* to the point at which, faced by that armed man, I uttered my *zufriedens diminuendo*, constantly more and more polite and respectful.

"Suddenly, red with fury, he summoned a second agent, and the two of them, foaming at the mouth, seized me firmly.

"Luck had it that while they were dragging me along, the Russian ambassador passed near us in his carriage. I saw his head as he recognized me thus flanked by two policemen.

"He had his carriage stopped and asked my guardians what was happening. After some explanations in German, those bravos let me go, not without many bows and excuses, the eloquence of which I grasped only because I saw their despairing gestures.

"The ambassador had me get into his carriage, where he told me that the police agent had, at the outset, simply asked me my name so that in case of need my testimony could be sought with regard to the crime that had been committed under my eyes. (Given that the agent, after all, was merely doing his duty, my innumerable *zufriedens* had exasperated him so much that he had taken me for a practical joker of a

" 'Furthermore,' I continued, 'you have done me too much honor by discussing my operas, I who am such a small matter alongside the great geniuses of your country. And I want to ask you to let me embrace you; and believe me that if my friendship has any value in your eyes, I offer it to you completely and with all my heart.' I embraced him effusively and saw a tear appear in his eyes."

WAGNER: "He was already suffering, I know, from the consumption that was to carry him off a short time later.

ROSSINI: "Exactly. To me he appeared to be in a pitiable state: with livid coloring, emaciated, racked by the consumptive's dry cough . . . limping, too. It pained one to see him. He came back to see me a few days later, to ask for some introductions for London, as he was about to go there. I was appalled by the idea of seeing him undertake such a journey. I tried very energetically to dissuade him, telling him that he would be committing a crime . . . suicide! It did no good. 'I know,' he answered, 'my life will end there . . . But I must do it. I must

---

sinister sort and had wanted to have the commissioner himself order me to respect the police.)

"The ambassador himself having said that I was to be excused because I did not understand German . . .

" 'This man? Not at all,' the agent had replied, 'he speaks the purest Viennese.'

" 'Be polite, then . . . and in pure Viennese at that.' "

go to stage *Oberon;* my contract obliges me to; I
must, I must . . .'

"Among other letters that I gave him for London—where I had formed some important relation-
ships during my stay in England—was a letter of
presentation to King George [IV], who, being
very gracious to artists, had been especially affable
with me. With a broken heart, I embraced that
great genius for the last time with the foreboding
that I should never see him again. That was only
too true. *Povero Weber!* *

". . . But we were discussing cabals," Rossini
went on. "This is my opinion on that subject: one
can do nothing about them except fight them with
silence and inertia; that is more effective, believe
me, than replies and anger. Ill will is legion; anyone
who wants to argue or—if you like it better—to
fight with that sow never will strike the last blow.
For my part, I spat on such attacks—the more they
buffeted me, the more I replied with *roulades;* I
fought sobriquets with my *triplets,* satires with my
pizzicati; and all the hurly-burly stirred up by
those who didn't like them never, I swear to you,
was able to make me give them one less blow on the
big drum in my *crescendos* or to prevent me, when

* Weber died in London during the night of July 5–6,
1826, aged thirty-nine, less than three months after the Covent Garden *première* of *Oberon.*

it suited me, from horrifying them with one more *felicità* in my finales. Believe me, the fact that you see me wearing a wig does not mean that those *b . . . utors* [9] succeeded in making me lose a single hair from my head."

Dumbfounded at first by this ultra-picturesque tirade, in which the Italian Maestro—until then solemn and reflective—had revealed himself suddenly under such a different aspect (Rossini in fact simply had returned to his natural, habitually jocular, humorous way of giving things their real names), Wagner could scarcely keep from laughing. "Oh, as for that," he answered (with a gesture toward his head), —"Thanks to what you had there, Maestro, that inertia of which you speak, wasn't it rather a real power; a power recognized by the public, and so sovereign that really one should have pitied the fools who risked opposing it? . . . But didn't I understand you to say a moment ago that you knew Beethoven?"

ROSSINI: "That's correct; at Vienna, precisely at the time I've just been telling you about, in 1822,

---

[9] When, during the course of the conversation, his mind brought up some memory or some natural difficulty that excited him, he thought little about framing his thought in academic language, but gave free voice to vocables of which it will be sufficient, I think, for me to underline the first letter; the rest will be divined.

when my opera *Zelmira* was presented there. I had heard quartets by Beethoven in Milan—I need not tell you with what a feeling of admiration! I also knew some of his piano works. In Vienna I attended for the first time a performance of one of his symphonies, the '*Eroica.*' That music bowled me over. I had only one thought: to meet that great genius, to see him, even if only once. I sounded out Salieri on the subject, knowing that he was on good terms with Beethoven."

WAGNER: "Salieri the composer of *Les Danaïdes?*" *

* Antonio Salieri (1750–1825) had studied with Gluck. When his opera *Les Danaïdes* was given its *première* at the Paris Opéra on April 26, 1784, it was billed as a collaboration by Gluck and himself. After its twelfth successful performance, however, Gluck issued a public statement that it had been composed entirely by Salieri. Its libretto—by François-Louis Gaud Lebland du Roullet and Louis-Théodore de Tschuddy—was partly an adaptation and partly a translation of *Ipermestra*, a text written for Gluck in 1778 by Raniero de' Calzabigi (though Gluck earlier—1744—had composed an *Ipermestra* to a libretto by Metastasio). After the first success of *Les Danaïdes*, Calzabigi sent the *Mercure de France* (August 21, 1784) a protest against its libretto's abuse of his auctorial rights. *Les Danaïdes* long remained a popular opera. At Trouville in 1855, Ferdinand Hiller mentioned Salieri to Rossini, who called him "that nice old gentleman" and added: "At that time he had a passion for composing canons. He came to our house for dessert almost every day. . . . We—my wife [Isabella Colbran], [Giovanni] David, and [Andrea] Nozzari, who usually dined with us—constituted quite a passable vocal

ROSSINI: "Exactly. In Vienna, where he had lived for a long time, he had attracted a lot of attention as the result of the vogue of several of his operas that were given at the Italian Theater; in fact, he told me that he sometimes saw Beethoven, but warned me that because of his [Beethoven's] distrustful and fantastic character, what I was asking for could not be arranged easily. Incidentally, Salieri had enjoyed equally good relations with Mozart. After the latter's death, it was suggested—and even seriously charged—that out of professional jealousy he had killed him by means of a slow poison . . ."

WAGNER: "That rumor still was current in Vienna in my time."

ROSSINI: "One day I amused myself by saying to Salieri as a joke: 'It's a lucky thing for Beethoven that, out of an instinct for self-preservation, he avoids having you at meals; for you might well send him wandering in the other world, as you did

---

quartet. Finally those never-ending canons made us quite dizzy, and we asked him to restrain himself a bit." Hiller remarked that Salieri's opera *Axur, re d'Ormus*, was among his earliest memories, and Rossini commented: "Like all his operas, it contains some excellent numbers. Though in *La Grotta di Trofonio* he certainly was surpassed by the poet: [Giovanni Battista] Casti's libretto is a real masterpiece. Poor Salieri! They blamed Mozart's death on him" (from Hiller's *Plaudereien mit Rossini*, vol. 2 of his *Aus dem Tonleben unserer Zeit* [Leipzig, 1868]).

Mozart.' 'Do I have the air of a poisoner, then?' Salieri replied. 'O, no!' I answered, 'you have more the air of a real craven! [*l'air d'un fieffé* c . . . ou-ard!]—which, in fact, he was. That poor devil, what is more, seemed to have little taste for passing as Mozart's assassin. What he couldn't swallow was that a Viennese journalist, a defender of German music—who liked Italian opera very little, and Salieri least of all—had written that 'unlike the *Dana-ïdes,* Salieri has emptied his cask in earnest and yet without much effort, never having had much in it.' Salieri's consternation over that was heartrending. Further, I must add, he could think of no better way of satisfying my desire than that of approaching [Giuseppe] Carpani,* the Italian poet, who

---

* Giuseppe Carpani (1752–1825), writer and editor, was a friend of Haydn, Mozart, and Beethoven. His monograph on Haydn (*Le Haydine, ovvero Lettere su la vita e le opere del celebre Giuseppe Haydn,* [Milan, 1812]) was plagiarized by Henri Beyle under his alternative pseudonym, Bombet (Paris, 1814). Carpani attacked the plagiarism in the pamphlet *Lettere dell'autore delle Haydine* (Vienna, 1815), which did not prevent Beyle from reprinting his plagiarism in 1817 under his more usual pseudonym, Stendhal (*Vies de Haydn, Mozart et Métastase*). Carpani was also the author of the libretto for Ferdinando Paër's popular opera *Camilla, ossia Il Sotterraneo* (Vienna, 1799) and of two pamphlets about Rossini: *Le Rossiniane, ossia Lettere musico-teatrali* (Padua, 1824) and *Lettera del Professore Giuseppe Carpani sulla musica di Gioacchino Rossini . . .* (Rome, 1826). Beethoven's arietta *In questa tomba oscura* is a setting of lines by Carpani.

was *persona grata* with Beethoven, and through whose intervention he felt sure of success. In fact, Carpani was so persistent with Beethoven that he extracted from him his consent to receive me.[10]

"Need I tell you? As I went up the stairs leading to the poor lodgings in which the great man lived, I had some difficulty in containing my emotion. When the door was opened, I found myself in a sort of hovel, so dirty as to testify to frightening disorder. I remember above all that the ceiling, which was immediately under the roof, was cracked, showing large crevices through which the rain must have come in waves.[11]

---

[10] Earlier, Rossini had told me that before he succeeded in seeing Beethoven through Carpani's intervention he had presented himself at the great composer's quarters spontaneously in the company of Artaria, the important publisher, who had been charged with introducing Rossini because he had constant relations with Beethoven. Rossini waited in the street; then Artaria came to tell him that Beethoven, being very unwell as the result of a cold that had affected his eyes, was not receiving anyone. It was probably this circumstance that led [Anton Felix] Schindler, Beethoven's biographer [*Biographie Ludwig van Beethovens*, 1840], to assert that he had refused to receive a visit from the Italian maestro. That day's situation had changed a few days later.

[11] This is perhaps the place to remark on some exaggeration in Rossini's account. Beethoven was then occupying with his nephew an agreeable enough apartment on the first floor of a house located in che Phargasse, in the Lehngrube neighborhood. The principal staircase, rather dark, opened onto a somewhat hidden ramshackle staircase, it is true,

"The Beethoven portraits that we know ren-
der the whole of his physiognomy faithfully

which led to a small room on the second floor which the
great composer had made into his workroom. Rossini was
taken into that room, which in fact could have led him to
think that he was in a garret mansard. (I have these details
directly from Ferdinand Hiller, who, during a stay in
Vienna shortly after Beethoven's death, often visited that
same apartment, then occupied by a tenant whom Hiller
knew intimately.) But that Beethoven's misery was extreme
at that time is undeniable; his biographers show us that. He
lived from day to day on borrowed money, which he tried
to obtain on all sides; for the sale of his manuscripts brought
him nothing: thirty to forty ducats at most for a piano
sonata!

enough. But what no burin would know how to express is the undefinable sadness spread across all his features, so that from under heavy eyebrows there shone, as if from the depths of caverns, two eyes which, though small, seemed to pierce you. The voice was soft and slightly fogged.*

"When we first entered, he paid no attention to us, but for some moments remained bent over a piece of printed music, which he was finishing correcting. Then, raising his head, he said to me brusquely in Italian that was comprehensible enough: 'Ah! Rossini, you are the composer of *Il Barbiere di Siviglia*? I congratulate you; it is an excellent *opera buffa;* I read it with pleasure, and it delights me. It will be played as long as Italian opera exists. Never try to do anything but *opera buffa;* wanting to succeed in another genre would be trying to force your destiny.'

"Carpani, who was with me (you must understand that he wrote out the words, and in German, there being no other way to pursue the conversation with Beethoven, whose words Carpani translated for me one after the other), interrupted

---

* Rossini is describing the fifty-one-year-old Beethoven of 1822, the year during which he labored ahead on the *Missa solemnis* (completed in 1823) and composed the C minor Piano Sonata, Opus 111.

immediately: 'But Maestro Rossini already has composed a large number of *opera seria* scores: *Tancredi, Otello, Mosè;* I sent them to you not long ago and suggested that you examine them.'

" 'In fact I have looked through them,' Beethoven replied. 'But look, *opera seria*—that's not the Italians' nature. They don't have enough musical science to deal with true drama; and how could they acquire it in Italy?' "

WAGNER: "That blow from the lion—it wouldn't have lightened Salieri's consternation if he had been there."

ROSSINI: "No, it certainly would not have! I told him about it later. He bit his lips . . . without hurting himself too much, I suppose, for, as I was about to tell you, he was timorous to the point at which I'm certain that in the otherworld the King of Hell, so as not to blush over the job of roasting such a coward, has had to have him sent elsewhere to be smoked! But to get back to Beethoven. 'In *opera buffa,*' he went on, 'nobody would have the wit to match you, you Italians. Your language and your vivacity of temperament destine you for it. Look at Cimarosa: how superior the comic part of his operas is to all the rest! It's the same with Pergolesi. You Italians, you make a great thing of his religious music, I know. I agree that there is very touching feeling in his *Stabat;* but its form lacks variety . . . the effect is monotonous; whereas *La Serva padrona*—' "

WAGNER (interrupting): "We must agree, Maestro (he said), that happily you refrained from taking Beethoven's advice . . ."

ROSSINI: "To tell you the truth, I really felt more aptitude for *opera buffa.* I preferred to treat comic rather than serious subjects. But I never had much choice among librettos, which were imposed upon me by the impresarios. I can't tell you how many times it happened that at first I received only part of the scenario, an act at a time, for which I had to compose the music without knowing what followed or the end of the subject. To think of it . . . what I had to do was earn a living for my father, my mother, and my grandmother! Going from town to town like a nomad, I wrote three, four operas a year. And don't think for a moment that all that earned me the means to act the *grand seigneur.* For *Il Barbiere* I received 1,200 francs, paid all at once, plus a hazel-colored suit with gold buttons which my impresario gave me so that I would be in a state to appear decently in the orchestra. That suit, it is true, may have been worth one hundred francs. Total: 1,300 francs. It had taken me only thirteen days to write that score. Taking everything into account, that came to a hundred francs per day. You see (Rossini added, smiling) that all the same I earned a big salary! I was very boastful to my father, who had earned only two francs fifty per day when he had the job of trumpet player at Pesaro."

WAGNER: "Thirteen days! That fact surely is unique. But, Maestro, I wonder how, under such conditions, shackled to that *vie de bohème* which you described, you were able to write those pages of *Otello*, of *Mosè*, superior pages that bear the mark, not of improvisation, but of thought-out labor after a concentration of all your mental forces!"

"Oh (Rossini interrupted) *I had facility and lots of instinct.*[12] Having to get along without a

---

[12] *J'avais de la facilité* . . . Most chroniclers, struck by this reply, which Wagner himself has reported, have thought to see in it some malicious intention, a spurt of malice imagined by the Monkey of Pesaro [*Singe de Pesaro*, burlesquing the sobriquet *cygne*—swan—*de Pesaro*] (as Rossini sometimes called himself) so as to have fun with the German master by persuading him to take this avowal at face value. . . . Nothing could be less exact; the same is true of the attitude attributed to Wagner by other publicists, that of having prostrated himself humbly before Rossini—confessing an outright *mea culpa* with regard to his doctrines.

The answer in question, I assert, was led up to quite naturally in the course of the conversation—as we just have seen—and could not leave any doubt behind as to its sincerity.

Furthermore, it is *true*. It is identical to the declaration really thorough musical education—and where, furthermore, *could* I have acquired it in Italy during my time?—I found in German scores the little that I know. An amateur at Bologna had some of them: *Die Schöpfung, Le Nozze di Figaro, Die Zauberflöte* . . . He lent them to me, and because at the age of fifteen I didn't have the means to import them from Germany, I copied them out tenaciously. I must tell you that I usually transcribed only the vocal part at first, without looking at the orchestral accompaniment. Then, on a separate sheet, I imagined an accompaniment of my own, which I later compared with Haydn's or Mozart's; after that I completed my copy by adding theirs. That system of working taught me more than all the courses at the Bologna Liceo. Ah! I feel that if I had been able to take my scholastic studies in your country I should have been able to produce something better than what is known of mine!"

WAGNER: "Surely not better—to cite only the *Scène des ténèbres* in your *Moïse*, the conspiracy in *Guillaume Tell*, or, of another sort, the *Quando Corpus morietur*. . ." *

---

that the Maestro was in the habit of making to his close friends when he talked to them about himself and his works.

* Wagner mentions the introductory chorus of *Moïse et Pharaon*, "*Dieu puissant du joug de l'impie*," dealing with the plague of shadows; the Act IV scene in *Guillaume Tell* in which, following Arnold's "*Amis, amis, secondez ma*

ROSSINI: "I'll have to concede that you have mentioned some happy episodes of my career. But what is all that alongside the work of Mozart, of a Haydn? I don't know how to tell you strongly enough how much I admire those masters for that supple science, that certainty which is so natural to

them in the art of composing. I have always envied them that; but it must be learned on the school benches, and one must also be a Mozart to know how to profit by it. As for Bach—not to leave your country—he is an overwhelming genius. If Beethoven is a prodigy of humanity, Bach is a miracle of God! I subscribed to the great publication of his

vengeance," those present conspire against Gessler; and a renowned section of the *Stabat Mater.*

works.* Look, you'll see it there, on my table, the last volume to appear. Can I tell you? The day when the next one arrives, that too will be an incomparably happy day for me. How I should like to hear a complete performance of his great [*Matthäus*] Passion before leaving this earth! But that's not to be dreamed of here among the French."

WAGNER: "It was Mendelssohn who first allowed the Germans to know the Passion, through the masterly performance that he himself conducted in Berlin."

ROSSINI: "Mendelssohn! O, what a sympathetic nature! I recall with pleasure the good hours that I spent in his company at Frankfurt in 1836. I found myself in that city on the occasion of a marriage that was being celebrated in the Rothschild family, and to which (I was living in Paris then) I had been invited. Ferdinand Hiller introduced me to Mendelssohn. How charmed I was to hear him play on the piano, among other things, some of his delicious *Lieder ohne Worte*! Then he played me some Weber. Then I asked him for Bach, plenty of Bach. Hiller had told me beforehand that no one interpreted [Bach] as well as he did. At first, Men-

---

* The Bach Gesellschaft, founded in 1850, was issuing what was intended to be a complete critical edition of Bach's music.

delssohn seemed stupefied by my request. 'How,' he asked, 'does it happen that you, an Italian, love German music so much?' 'I don't love any other kind,' I answered; then I added, in a somewhat too offhanded way: 'As for Italian music, I don't give a damn for it!' He looked at me in perplexity, which didn't prevent him from playing admirably and

with rare good nature several fugues and other pieces by the great Bach. I heard from Hiller that after we parted, Mendelssohn, recalling my sally, said to him: 'This Rossini, is he really serious? In any case, he's a very odd fish.' "

WAGNER (laughing heartily): "Maestro, I can understand Mendelssohn's stupefaction; but will you allow me to ask you how your visit to Beethoven ended?"

ROSSINI: "Oh, it was short. You understand that one whole side of the conversation had to be written out. I told him of all my admiration for his genius, all my gratitude for his having allowed me an opportunity to express it to him.

"He replied with a profound sigh and exactly these words: '*Oh! un infelice!*' After a pause he asked me for some details about the Italian opera houses, about famous singers, whether or not Mozart's operas were performed frequently, if I was satisfied with the Italian troupe at Vienna.

"Then, wishing me a good performance and success for *Zelmira*, he got up, led us to the door, and said to me again: 'Above all, make a lot of *Barbers*.'

"Going down that ramshackle staircase, I felt such a painful impression of my visit to that great man—thinking of that destitution, that privation—that I couldn't hold back my tears. 'Ah!' Carpani said, 'that's the way he wants it. He is a misanthrope, morose, and doesn't know how to hold on to a single friendship.'

"That very evening I attended a gala dinner given by Prince [Klemens von] Metternich. Still completely upset by that visit, by that lugubrious '*Un infelice!*' which remained in my ears, I couldn't, I assure you, protect myself against a feeling of inner confusion at seeing, by comparison, myself treated with such regard by that brilliant Viennese assemblage; that led me to say stoutly and without any discretion at all what I thought about the conduct of the Court and the aristocracy toward the greatest genius of the epoch, who needed so little and was abandoned to such distress. They gave me the very reply that I had received from Carpani. I demanded to know, however, if Beethoven's deafness didn't deserve the greatest pity, if it was really charitable to bring up again the weaknesses for which they were reproaching him, to seek reasons for refusing to go to his assistance. I added that it would be so easy, by drawing up a very small subscription, to assure him an income large enough to place him beyond all need for the rest of his life. That proposal didn't win the support of a single person.[13]

"After dinner, the evening ended with a reception that brought to Metternich's salons the greatest names in Vienna society. There was also a

---

[13] This indifference—almost criminal—which Viennese society persisted in vis-à-vis Beethoven and the precarious situation weighing upon him, is the more inexplicable in view of the fact that at this time the Master's published works had reached the number 111 in the catalogue, and therefore included the symphonies 1 through 7, *Fidelio*, quartets, trios, almost all of the works for piano, etc. And we must add that on their appearance, all these masterpieces, far from being misprized, enjoyed universal admiration.

concert. One of Beethoven's most recently published trios figured on the program—always he, he everywhere, as was said of Napoleon. The new masterpiece was listed to religiously and won a splendid success. Hearing it amid all that worldly magnificence, I told myself sadly that perhaps at that moment the great man was completing—in the isolation of the hovel in which he lived—some work of high inspiration which was destined, like his earlier works, to initiate into beauties of a sublime order that same brilliant aristocracy from which he was being excluded, and which, amid all its pleasures, was not at all disquieted by the misery of the man who supplied it with those pleasures.

"Not having succeeded in my attempts to create an annual income for Beethoven, I didn't lose courage immediately. I wanted to try to get together sufficient funds to buy him a place to live. I did succeed in obtaining some promises to subscribe; but even when I added my own, the final result was very mediocre. So I had to abandon that second project. Generally I got this answer: 'You don't know Beethoven well. The day after he became the owner of a house, he would sell it again. He never would know how to adjust himself to a fixed abode; for he feels the need to change his quarters every six months and his servant every six weeks.' Was that a way to get rid of me?

"But that's enough, I think, about me and the others who are the Past [*Passé*], even the Dead [*Trépassé*]. Let's talk about the Present and, if you'll permit it, *monsieur Wagner*, above all about the *Future*, as in any discussion your name always appears to be inseparable from that epithet. This, be it understood, without the least malicious intention on my part.—And, to begin with, tell me, are you planning to stay in Paris? As for your opera *Tannhäuser*, I'm sure that you will succeed in having it produced. There has been too much talk about that work for the Parisians to be able to stifle their curiosity about hearing it. Is the translation finished?"

WAGNER: "It is not finished yet; I am working on it actively with a collaborator who is very able and, above all, extremely patient. This is a question—for perfect understanding of the musical expression—of identifying, to put it this way, each French word with the corresponding sense of the German word, and under the same notation. It is hard work and very difficult to accomplish."

ROSSINI: "But why, in the manner of Gluck, Spontini, Meyerbeer, don't you start from the beginning by writing an opera with all the numbers adapted to a French libretto? * Wouldn't you then

---

* This was, of course, the procedure that Rossini himself had followed when transforming the Italian *Maometto II*

be in a position to take into consideration the taste predominating here and the special atmosphere of theatrical matters inherent in the French spirit?"

WAGNER: "In my case, Maestro, I don't think that that could be done. After *Tannhäuser*, I wrote *Lohengrin*, then *Tristan und Isolde*. These three operas, from both the literary and the musical points of view, represent a logical development in my conception of the definitive and absolute form of the lyric drama. My style has undergone the inevitable effects of that gradation. And if it is true that now I sense the possibility of writing other works in the style of *Tristan*, I swear that I am incapable of taking up my *Tannhäuser* manner again. Well, then, if I were in the position of having to compose an opera for Paris on a French text, I could not and should not follow any other road than the one that has led me to the composition of *Tristan*.

"Further, such a work as that, comprising such a disturbance of the traditional forms of opera, certainly would remain unappreciated and would have no chance, under present conditions of being accepted by the French."

ROSSINI: "And tell me, what in your mind has been the point of departure for these reforms?"

(1820) into the French *Le Siège de Corinthe* (1826), *Mosè in Egitto* (1818) into *Moïse et Pharaon* (1827).

WAGNER: "Their system was not developed all at once. My doubts go back to my first attempts, which did not satisfy me; and it was rather in the poetic conception than in the musical conception that the germ of these reforms suddenly entered my mind. My first works, in fact, had above all a literary objective. Later, preoccupied with means to use for enlarging the significance by the very penetrating addition of musical expression, I deplored the way in which the independence with which my thought was moving in the visionary realm was decreased by the demands imposed by routine in the forms of the musical drama.[14]

"Those bravura *arias*, those insipid duets fatally manufactured on the same model, and how many other hors d'oeuvre that interrupt the stage action without reason! then the *septets*! for in every respectable opera it was necessary to have a solemn septet in which the characters of the drama, setting the meaning of their roles aside, formed a line across the front of the stage—all reconciled!—to come to a common accord * (of often what accords, good Lord!) so as to supply the public with one of those stale banalities . . ."

ROSSINI (interrupting): "And do you know

---

[14] One should not lose sight of the fact that Wagner was born in 1813.

* See translator's footnote, page 33.

what we called that in Italy in my time? *The row of artichokes.* I assure you that I was perfectly aware of the silliness of the thing. It always gave me the impression of a line of porters who had come to sing in order to earn a tip. But what would you have had me do? It was the custom—a conces-

sion that one had to make to the public, which otherwise would have thrown sliced potatoes at us . . . or even ones that hadn't been sliced!"

WAGNER (continuing without paying much attention to Rossini's interruption): "And as for the orchestra, those routine accompaniments . . . colorless . . . obstinately repeating the same formulas without taking into account the diversity of the characters and situations. . . . in a word, all that concert music, foreign to the action, without any reason for being there except the *convention*—music that obstructs the most famous operas in many places . . . all that seemed to me something contrary to good sense and incompatible with the high mission of an art noble and worthy of that name."

ROSSINI: "Among other things, you just referred to the bravura arias. Well, what do you suppose? That was my nightmare. To satisfy at the same time the prima donna, the first tenor, the first bass! . . . those jolly fellows existed—without forgetting, above all, the qualifying *terrible feminine*—who thought it wise to count the number of measures in one of their arias, then come to me to declare that they wouldn't sing because another of their colleagues had an aria containing several measures more, not to mention a larger number of trills, of ornaments . . ."

WAGNER (gaily): "It was measured by a ruler! nothing was left for the composer to do but take a musical *meter* as collaborator for his inspirations."

ROSSINI: "Let's just call it an aria-meter! Really, when I think of those people, they were wild animals. There you have the only people who, having made my head sweat, soon made me bald. But let's leave that and go on with your reasoning . . .

"In effect, and without replying, it seems to me to deal with the rational, rapid, and regular development of the dramatic action. Only—that independence claimed by the literary conception, how to maintain it in alliance with that of musical form, which is nothing but *convention?*—you yourself used the word! For if one must obey the sense of complete logic, it goes without saying that when speaking, one does not sing; an angry man, a conspirator, a jealous man does not sing! (humorously): An exception, perhaps, for lovers, whom, in a strict sense, one can have *coo* . . . But, even more forceful: does one go to one's death singing? *Convention* in the opera, then, from beginning to end. And the instrumentation itself? . . . Who, then, when an orchestra is unleashed, could pinpoint the difference in the description of a storm, a riot, a fire? . . . always convention!"

WAGNER: "Clearly, Maestro, *convention*—and in very large supply—is imposed upon one, for otherwise one would have to do away completely with the lyric drama and even the comedy in music. It is none the less indisputable, however, that this convention, having been raised to the level of a form of art, must be understood in a way to avoid excesses leading to the absurd, the ridiculous. And there you have the abuse against which I am reacting. But they have wanted to muddy my thought. Don't they represent me as an arrogant man . . . denigrating Mozart?"

ROSSINI (with a touch of humor): *"Mozart, l'angelo della musica . . .* But who, short of sacrilege, would dare to touch him?"

WAGNER: "I have been accused, as if it were a mere trifle, of repudiating all existing operatic music—with rare exceptions, such as Gluck and Weber. They refuse, clearly with closed minds, to want to understand my writings. And in what a way! But, far from denying or not myself feeling, even to the highest degree, the charm—*as pure music*—of lots of admirable pages in justly famous operas, it is against the role of that music when it is condemned to be used as a purely diverting hors d'oeuvre, or where, a slave to routine and foreign to the stage action, it is not addressed systematically to anything but the ear's sensuality—it is against that role that I rise up and want to react.

"In my view, an opera, being destined by its complex essence to have as its aim that of forming an organism concentrating the perfect union of all the arts that contribute to making it—the poetic art, the musical art, the decorative and plastic art—isn't this a disparagement of the musician's mission, this desire to confine him to being the simple instrumental illustrator of just any libretto, which imposes upon him in advance a summary number of arias, duets, scenes, ensembles . . . in a word, of *pieces* (pieces—that is to say, things cut up in the true sense of the word) which he must translate into notes almost like a colorist filling in proofs printed in black? Certainly there are many examples of composers inspired by a moving dramatic situation who have written immortal pages. But how many other pages of their scores are diminished or nullified because of the vicious system I am pointing out! Well, as long as these follies persist, as long as one does not sense the prevalence of complete reciprocal penetration by music and poem or that *double conception* based, from the beginning, upon a single thought, the true music drama does not exist."

ROSSINI: "That is to say, if I understand you correctly, that in order to realize your ideal, the composer must be his own librettist? That seems to me, for many reasons, to be an insurmountable condition."

WAGNER (very animated): "And why? What reason is there against having composers, while they are learning counterpoint, study literature at the same time, search history, read legends? Which would lead them instinctively thereafter to attach themselves to a subject, poetic or tragic, related to their own temperament? . . . And then, if they lack ability or experience for arranging the dramatic intrigue, wouldn't they then have the resource of going to some practiced dramatist with whom they could identify themselves in a steadily maintained collaboration?

"Furthermore, there have been few dramatic composers, I think, who have not at times instinctively displayed remarkable literary and poetic aptitudes: rearranging or refashioning to their own taste either the text or the arrangement of a given scene which they have felt differently and understood better than their librettists. Not to go farther afield, you yourself, Maestro—let us take, for example, the scene of the oath swearing in *Guillaume*

Tell—would you say that you followed servilely, word by word, the text given you by your collaborators? I don't believe it. It is not difficult, when one looks at that closely, to discover in many places effects of declamation and of gradation which bear such an imprint of *musicality* (if I may say it that way), of *spontaneous inspiration*, that I refuse to attribute their genesis exclusively to the intervention of the textual scheme that was before your eyes. A librettist, whatever his ability, cannot know—above all, in scenes complicated by ensembles—how to conceive the arrangement that will suit the composer when he is creating the musical fresco as his imagination will suggest it."

ROSSINI: "What you say is true. That scene, in fact, was profoundly modified to my specifications, and not without trouble. I composed *Guillaume Tell* at the country home of my friend Aguado,* where I was spending the summer. There my librettists were not at hand. But Armand Marrast and [Adolphe] Crémieux ** (parenthetically, *two future conspirators* against the government of

---

* Alejandro María Aguado, Marqués de las Marismas, a naturalized Frenchman of Spanish birth, was a man of great wealth and a very generous patron of Rossini.

** Armand Marrast, writer and publicist, was a political figure of some importance who served as mayor of Paris and president of the National Assembly. Adolphe Crémieux was an outstanding lawyer and politician.

Louis-Philippe), who were also staying at Aguado's in the country, came to my assistance with
changes in the text and the versification which I
needed in order to work out, as I had to, the plan of
my own conspirators against Gessler."

WAGNER: "There, Maestro, you have an im-
plicit confession that already confirms in part what
I have just been saying; it would be enough to
enlarge that principle to establish that my ideas are
not so contradictory, so impossible to realize, as
they may seem at first.

"I assert that it is logically inevitable that, by
an entirely natural evolution, perhaps a slow
one—there will be born, not that *music of the future* which they insist upon attributing to me the
pretension of wanting to give birth to all by myself, but the *future of the music drama*, in which
the general movement will play a part and from
which will arise an orientation—as fecund as it will
be new—in the concept of *composers, singers*, and
public."

ROSSINI: "In short, it is a radical revolution!
And do you think that the *singers*—let's talk about
them right away—habituated to displaying their
talent in virtuosity, which will be replaced—if I
divine clearly—by a sort of *declamatory recitative*,
do you think that the *public*, habituated to—let's
use the word—the *vieux jeu*, will finally submit to

changes so destructive of the entire past? I doubt it strongly."

WAGNER: "There will certainly be a slow education to achieve, but it will be achieved. As for the public, does it shape the masters, or do the masters shape the public? Another situation in which I see you as an illustrious demonstration.

"Wasn't it, in fact, your very personal manner that made people in Italy forget all your predecessors; that acquired for you with unheard of rapidity an unexampled popularity? Well, Maestro, your influence, once it had passed the frontier, didn't it become universal?

"As for the singers, whose resistance you raised to me as an objection, they will have to submit, to accept a situation that, what is more, will elevate them. When they have understood that the lyric drama in its new form will furnish them, not, it is true, with the elements of easy success owing either to the strength of their lungs or to the advantages of a charming voice—they will understand that nevertheless the art demands a much higher mission from them. Forced to stop isolating themselves inside the personal limitations of their role, they will identify themselves with both the philosophic and the esthetic spirit dominating the work. They will live, if I may express myself this way, in an atmosphere in which—*everything con-*

tributing to the whole—nothing should remain secondary. Further, broken of the habit of ephemeral success through fleeting virtuosity, delivered from the torment of having to expend their voices on insipid words lined up in banal rhymes—they will understand how it will have become possible for them to be able to surround their names with a more glorious and durable aureole when they will be incarnating the characters they represent by complete penetration—from the psychological and human point of view—of their *raison d'être* in the drama; when they will base themselves on deepened studies of the ideas, customs, character of the period in which the action occurs; when they will join irreproachable diction to the prestige of masterly declamation, full of truth and nobility."

ROSSINI: "From the point of view of *pure art*, those are unquestionably long views, seductive perspectives. But from the point of view of musical form in particular, it is, as I said, the fatal blow to declamatory melody—*the funeral oration of melody*! Otherwise, how ally expressive notation, to say it that way, of each syllable of the language to the melodic form, in which precise rhythms and symmetrical concord among the constituent elements must establish the physiognomy?"

WAGNER: "Certainly, Maestro, such a system if applied and pushed with such rigor would be

6 7

intolerable. But here, if you want to understand me clearly: far from brushing melody aside, on the contrary, I demand it, and *copiously*. Isn't melody the vitality of every musical organism? Without melody, nothing is or could be. Only, let us understand one another: I require it not to be that melody which, shut up inside the narrow limitations of conventional procedures, submits to the yoke of symmetrical periods, persistent rhymes, foreseen harmonic progressions, obligatory cadences. I want melody *free, independent,* unfettered. A melody particularizing by its own characteristic contour not only each character in such a way that he cannot be confused with another, but also each event, each episode inherent in the context of the drama. A melody of very precise form which, while conforming to the sense of the poetic text by its multiple inflections, can extend itself, contract itself, prolong itself [15] according to the conditions required by the musical effect that the composer wants to obtain. And as for that sort of melody, Maestro, you stereotyped a sublime specimen in the scene of *Guillaume Tell,* '*Sois immobile,*' where

---

[15] "A melody in the battle [*mélodie de combat*]," Rossini added quickly. But Wagner, carried away by what he was saying, paid no attention to that really droll interruption. I pointed it out to him later. "For a *charge*," he exclaimed, "and behold, at least one that is led in a good corner of the mind. Ah! I'll remember that: *mélodie de combat* . . . A lucky hit!"

the very freedom of the singing line, accentuating each word and sustained by the breathing strokes of the violoncellos, reached the highest summits of lyric expression."

ROSSINI: "So I made *music of the future* without knowing it?"

WAGNER: "There, Maestro, you made music of all times, and that is the best."

ROSSINI: "I'll tell you that the feeling that moved me most during my life was the love that I felt for my mother and my father, and which they repaid me at usurious rates, I am happy to tell you.

It was there, I think, that I found the tone that I needed for the scene of the *apple*—in *Guillaume Tell*.*

"But one more question, *monsieur Wagner*, if you'll permit me: how to fit into this system the simultaneous employment of two, or several, voices, as well as that of choruses? Should one, so as to be logical, forbid them? . . ."

WAGNER: "In fact, it would be rigorously logical to model musical dialogue on spoken dialogue, assigning speech to the characters one after the other. But on the other hand, one also admits that, for example, two different people can find themselves in the same spiritual state at a given moment—sharing a common feeling and, as a result, joining their voices to identify themselves in a single thought. In the same way, several assembled characters, if there is a discussion involving diverse feelings animating them, can sensibly use the means of expressing them simultaneously while each one determines individually what is his own.

"And do you understand now, Maestro, what immense resources, infinite, are offered to composers by this system of applying to each personage of

---

* In the finale of Act III of *Guillaume Tell*, before shooting the apple from his son's head, Tell orders the boy to kneel and pray motionlessly (*"Sois immobile, et vers la terre incline un genou suppliant"*).

the drama, to each situation—a typical melodic for-
mula susceptible—while preserving its original
character—of lending itself to the most varying,
the most extended developments during the course
of the action? . . .

"Further, these ensembles, in which each of
the characters appears in his own individuality, but
in which these elements are combined in a polyphony appropriate to the action—these ensembles
no longer will present the spectacle, I repeat, of
those absurd ensembles in which characters animated by the most contradictory passions find
themselves, at a given moment, condemned without rhyme or reason to unite their voices in a sort
of *largo d'apothéose*, in which the patriarchal har-
monies make one think only 'that one cannot be
better than in the bosom of his family.' [16]

"As for choruses," Wagner continued, "this is
a psychological truth: that the collective masses
obey a determined sensation more energetically
than the isolated man—such as dread, fury, pity
. . . Then it is logical to admit that the crowd can
express such a state collectively in the sound-lan-
guage of the opera without shocking good sense.
Further still, the intervention of choruses, granted

---

[16] An allusion to the very popular finale [*"On ne saurait
être mieux qu'au sein de sa famille"*] of *Lucile*, an opera by
Grétry.

that it be indicated logically in the situations of the drama, is a power without equal and one of the most precious agents of theatrical effect. Among a hundred examples, shall I recall the impression of anguish in the vivid chorus in *Idomeneo*—*'Corriamo, fuggiamo!'*—not to forget, either, Maestro, the admirable fresco in your *Moïse*—*the so desolate chorus of the shades?* . . ."

ROSSINI: "Again! (striking his forehead, and very amusingly), decidedly, then, I had—me too—some disposition toward the *music of the future?* . . . You are salving my wounds! If I were not too old, I'd start over, and then . . . let the *ancien régime* beware!"

"Ah, Maestro—Wagner replied at once—if you had not laid down your pen after *Guillaume Tell* at thirty-seven years—a crime! you yourself have no idea of everything that you could have extracted from that brain there! At that time, you had done no more than begin . . ."

ROSSINI (again becoming serious): "What should I have done? I had no children. Had I had any, I doubtless would have continued to work. But, to tell you the truth, after having worked and composed forty operas during fifteen years of that so lazy period, I felt a need to rest and I returned to Bologna to live in peace.*

---

* In January, 1866, Rossini—then nearly seventy-four and looking back thirty-seven years to his abandonment of opera

"Also, the condition of the Italian theaters, which already during my career left much to be desired, then was in full decay; the art of singing had darkened. That was to be foreseen."

WAGNER: "To what do you attribute such an unexpected phenomenon in a country in which beautiful voices are superabundant?"

ROSSINI: "To the disappearance of the *castrati*. One can form no notion of the charm of voice and consummate virtuosity—which, lacking something else, and by a charitable compensation—those best of the best possessed. They were also incomparable teachers. The teaching of singing in the master schools attached to the churches and supported at the churches' expense generally was confided to them. Some of those schools were famous. They were real singing academies. The pupils flocked to them, and some of them abandoned the choir loft to devote themselves to theatrical careers. But after

---

—was to write to Giovanni Pacini: "Dear Giovanni, be at peace; keep in mind my philosophic intention to abandon my Italian career in 1822, my French in 1829; this foresightedness is not given to all; God accorded it to me, and I always bless him." It had not, of course, been that simple, and elsewhere in the same letter, as if still feeling some need to justify to others his retirement from operatic composition, Rossini speaks of music as "this art which has as its only basis the ideal and feeling," adding that it could not be separated from "the influence of the times in which we live. Today, the ideal and feeling are directed exclusively toward *steam, rapine,* and the barricades. . . ."

a new political regime was installed throughout Italy by my restless contemporaries, the master schools were suppressed, being replaced by some *conservatories* in which, though good traditions existed, absolutely nothing of *bel canto* was conserved.

"As to the *castrati*, they vanished, and the usage disappeared in the creation of new customs. That was the cause of the irretrievable decay of the art of singing. When it had disappeared, *opera buffa* (the best that we had) was cast adrift. And *opera seria?* Audiences, who even in my time showed themselves not very likely to rise to the height of that great art, showed no interest in that sort of spectacle. The announcement of an *opera seria* on the posters usually resulted in attracting some plethoric spectators wanting to breathe in a cooling aria * remote from the crowd. There you have the reasons—and there were others too—why I judged that I had something better to do, which was to keep silent. I committed suicide, and *così finita la comedia* [*sic*]."

Rossini rose, clasped Wagner's hands affectionately, and added: "My dear *monsieur Wagner*, I don't know how to thank you enough for your call, and particularly for the exposition of

---

* A pun on the Italian word *aria*, which means both air and one sort of vocal solo.

your ideas, so clear and so interesting, which you have been kind enough to give me. I who no longer compose, being at the age at which, rather, one *decomposes* while waiting to be *re-decomposed* truly—I am too old to being looking toward new horizons; but your ideas—whatever your detractors may say—are of a sort to make the young reflect. Of all the art, music, because of its ideal essence, is the one most exposed to transformations. They are without limits. After Mozart, could one have foreseen Beethoven? After Gluck, Weber? And the end certainly is not after them. Each one must strive, if not to advance, at least to discover the new without worrying about the legend of a certain Hercules, a great traveler toward the visible, who reached a certain spot at which he could no longer see very clearly and, it is said, set up a column and then retraced his steps."

WAGNER: "Was it perhaps a private hunting stake, to prevent others from going farther on?"

ROSSINI: "*Chi lo sa?* Doubtless you are right, for one is assured that he displayed a brave predilection for hunting lions. Let us hope, however, that our art never will be limited by a placer of that sort of column. For my part, I belonged to my time. To others, in particular to you whom I see vigorous and impregnated with such masterly tendencies, falls the creation of what is new and comes next—which I wish you with all my heart."

Thus ended that memorable interview, during which, for the long half hour that it lasted, these two men—in whom the intellectual verve of the one did not leave in peace the humorous repartee of the other—never, as I can attest, showed the slightest sign of being bored.

Rossini, while conducting us back through the dining room next to his chamber, suddenly stopped in front of a delightful small piece of furniture in fine marqueterie placed between the two windows and familiar to all habitués of his salons. It was a small mechanical organ of the seventeenth century, of Florentine manufacture.

"Look"—the Maestro said to Wagner—"this little organ is going to let you hear some old airs from my country which may perhaps interest you." He touched the spring, and at once the instrument supplied, in old-time flageolet sound, its whole repertoire. That consisted of short popular airs.

"What do you think of it?"—Rossini asked—"there is some of the past, even of the dead. It is simple and naïve. Who was the unknown composer? Some fiddler, it would seem. It dates from long ago unquestionably, and it still lives! Will as much remain of us in a century?"

Of us! Certain hair splitters have not failed to use the chance to see here, in this remark to Wagner, a sharp thrust disguised under the semblance of senile bonhomie. That was not, I think, the Maestro's intention. That reflection—which, what is more, was identical to remarks that I had heard him make in the same reference on other occasions, was spoken simply, without *arrière-pensée*, apparently on the spur of the moment.[17] Wagner paid no attention to it.

Then we bade farewell to the Maestro.

---

[17] This recalls to me that one evening after dinner, the Maestro, having done the honors of the little organ for Auber, said to him: "*Voilà!* If in fifty years some similar mechanism still sounds forth my '*Di tanti palpiti*' [in *Tancredi*], that, I am sure, will be all that will remain of me." AUBER: "And your *Barbiere*? Do you believe that it won't be played in a century, and in all the centuries?" ROSSINI: "Before half a century has passed, all of our music probably will be Chinese, as the political high hats assure us that the Asiatic peril is already approaching the antechamber of Europe. You undoubtedly will still be living (Auber was almost ninety), seeing that you are determined to *conserve* yourself in order, I suppose, to justify your title as Director of the *Conservatory;* then you will have the satisfaction of hearing your *Cheval de bronze* in Chinese, after which celestial and piquant Mandarins certainly will rejuvenate your fiber by provoking new and perhaps heroic variations as an epilogue to those in *Les Diamants de la couronne*." AUBER: "As for the Chinese, I adore the little feet, but not so much that this . . ." ROSSINI: "As a musician you are mistaken, for these damsels don't know how to regulate their steps except by means of *appoggiature*." AUBER: "Redoubled steps [*des pas redoublés*] to the Chinese maidens, then!" And so forth.

Going down the stairs, Wagner said to me: "I swear to you that I did not expect to find in Rossini the man who appeared before me. He is simple, natural, serious, and shows himself quick to take an interest in all the points that I touched upon during this short talk. I couldn't set forth in a few words all the ideas that I develop in my writing about the conception that I have formed of the necessary evolution of the lyric drama toward new destinies. I have had to restrict myself to some general views, making use of practical details only when that could make my point immediately. But, be that as it may, it was to be expected that my assertions would seem excessive to him, given the systematic spirit that prevailed when he made his career and with which he necessarily remains deeply imbued today. Like Mozart, he possessed melodic inventiveness to the highest degree. Further, that was marvelously seconded by his instinct for the stage and for dramatic expression. What mightn't he have produced if he had been given a strong, complete musical education? especially if, less Italian and less skeptical, he had felt inside him the religion of his art? There can be no doubt that he would have taken off on a flight that would have raised him to the highest peaks. In a word, he is a genius who was led astray by not having been well prepared and not having found the milieu for which his high creative abilities had designed him. But I must declare: of all the musicians whom I have met in Paris, *he alone is truly great.*"

Having left Wagner and gone home immediately, I hastened to put into order the notes that I had taken during the conversation of these two celebrated men.

I now make this comment: that Rossini, who had regaled us so emotionally with his visit to Beethoven while expressing all the admiration that he felt for that colossal genius, was far from doubting that he had a colossus of the same stamp before him.

Wagner, let us not forget, had not yet conquered the prestige that celebrity confers. His name, though it already was spreading across Germany after performances of *Tannhäuser* and *Lohengrin* in various theaters, had—it is true—acquired notoriety in Paris; but it was the polemicist rather than the musician who was in view in the numerous usually hostile articles that the press was multiplying against him. From that resulted the fact that in the eyes of Rossini—who was not familiar with any of Wagner's music—Wagner, in short, then occupied as a personality a position much below that of a Gounod, a Félicien

David *—perhaps represented, rather, the type of Teuton who intoxicates himself on the suggestions of an exalted brain, more talker than musician, too radical in his renovating utopias for anyone to believe seriously in the possibility of their realization. At first, therefore, Rossini had listened to Wagner with the appearance of polite curiosity rather than with the marks of lively, concentrated interest. During the course of the talk, Rossini's impression was modified, his perspicacity being well known, and he was not long in perceiving that this Teuton was *a brain.*

Furthermore, that meeting between these two men of genius, of whom the one, sated with fame, had survived the most brilliant of careers for thirty years; of whom the other, on the eve of an incomparable glory, had not yet revealed to his contemporaries everything that his titanic faculties concealed; that interview was what it should have been: courtly and simple on the part of Rossini, dignified and full of deference on the part of Wagner.

The latter, when presenting himself before the Pesaro master, had no illusions, as goes without

---

* Félicien David (1810–1876) had become famous in Paris in 1844 with his symphonic ode *Le Désert,* which was played at the Salle Ventadour for an entire month, and in 1851 with his opera *La Perle du Brésil.*

saying, about the welcome that a setting-forth of his doctrines would receive. He did not even expect that Rossini would put so much urbanity into prolonging their talk; and the cry of alarm: *but it is the funeral oration of melody which you pronounce there,* did not at all surprise him. It was the *cri du coeur* that he could not have failed to foresee. Also, it was not with the intention of being understood that Wagner had asked for the interview; but above all in the hope of being able to study psychologically at close range this strange musician, miraculously endowed, who, after so astonishingly swift a rise in the development of his creative faculties—from which *Guillaume Tell* finally emerged—then, at the age of thirty-seven, had had nothing more urgent [to do] than to separate himself from his genie as one disembarrasses oneself of an encumbering burden, in order to bury himself in the bourgeois *farniente* of a colorless life without worrying more about his art than if he never had practiced it. That was the phenomenon that attracted Wagner's curiosity, and which he wanted to be able to analyze.

Also, it could only please him to seize the occasion to protest in person against the absurdities that an ignorant and aggressive press attributed to him on the subject of his purported feelings of disdain for the operatic music of the most illustrious masters, his predecessors, with Mozart at the head, Meyerbeer and Rossini following. To this last—as we have just seen—he made [the denial] in dignified and precise terms, restricting himself to a simple denial, as was fitting for a man who did not have to free himself of imputations spread abroad by malice or of allegations that his declarations were consciously false.

Furthermore, absolved when, in the presence of the Italian master, he set forth his ideas in their real significance, he did not embarrass himself with either oratorical precautions or ambiguous subterfuges; even less did he dream of mitigating them by means of restrictions smelling of court holy water while he was categorically formulating his criticism of the defective, worm-eaten secular organism of the opera and the vicious system that composers employed to ornament their music. It must be agreed that this arrow was only slightly blunted as shot directly toward Rossini.

The latter, as we have seen, was far from taking umbrage; he talked courteously in the sprightly, humorous tone habitual with him. But, noticing the change that little by little came over his attitude, one clearly perceived, I repeat, that he had not been slow to understand the real value of his visitor. Rather than a visionary bursting with self-sufficience and rambling on in the confused phraseology of incoherent pedantry—which Rossini's entourage had pictured this German as being—he soon understood that he had before him an intelligence of the first order, robust, clear, conscious of its strength, capable of taking an eagle's eye view of the unlimited spaces of the art of music and resolved to raise itself into their highest reaches.

All equivocation having been dissipated quickly, the meeting of these two men, then, had led to a reciprocal feeling of esteem which persisted thereafter with as much sincerity as deference. And yet, how disparate these two geniuses!

Wagner utterly Germanic in temperament, absolute, imperious, combative, nourished by the school of Schopenhauer, as profound and sublime as Beethoven, a brain perpetually at the boil, dominated and tormented by his *Genius*, his *Demon*, as he called it; conscious of his apostolate, which was his strength, and conscious of his duty to create, which was his destiny.

The other, Rossini, the Italian, an alert spirit, brilliant, adept in the philosophy of Epicurus, enjoying the surfaces of things rather than taking the trouble to penetrate deeply: letting himself live from day to day while tossing improvisations to all the winds, having as a *Genius*, in lieu of Wagner's ravaging *Demon*, a sweet and generous fairy full of caresses; not succumbing to the allurements of his art except when constrained to, and then appealing to the complaisance of a marvelous instinct always ready to respond to his solicitations.

Such was the contrast between these two musicians, of whom the one, in the course of a tempestuous life, had to fight to the end, to create up to his last breath; of whom the other, having completed the first period of an existence crowded with triumphs and delights, rested from the seventh luster of his age, satisfied with himself and his work, just as the Eternal rested on the seventh day of the Creation.

So I put my notes in order, and that same evening, as usual, went to Rossini's, where one always was sure to meet some interesting people. There I found, among others, AZEVEDO,* a music critic attached to the paper *L'Opinion nationale*, a fanatic Rossinist and one of Wagner's most violent persecutors.

Seeing him, Rossini addressed him banteringly: "Eh, Azevedo, well! I saw him, he came . . . the monster . . . your *bête noire* . . . Wagner!"

While the Maestro then went on to talk with Carafa,** Azevedo took me aside to obtain some details about that interview. But Rossini came up and interrupted us an instant later. "You talked in vain"—he went on, addressing Azevedo—"this Wagner—I must confess—seems to me to be en-

---

* Alexis-Jacob Azevedo (1813–1875), long familiar to readers of *Le Ménestrel*, Paris, wrote for its publisher what was for many years the standard Rossini biography: *G. Rossini: Sa Vie et ses œuvres* (Paris, 1864).

** Michele Enrico Carafa, Principe di Colobrano (1787–1872), was a prolific composer of operas and lifetime friend of Rossini, whom he assisted in the completion of both *Mosè in Egitto* and *Adelaide di Borgogna*, and for whom he prepared the Paris Opéra version (1860) of *Semiramide*.

dowed with first-class faculties. His whole physique—his chin most of all—reveals an iron-willed temperament. It's a great thing to know how to *will*. If he possesses the gift of *being able* in the same degree, as I believe he does, he will get himself talked about."

Azevedo fell silent; but he whispered in my ear: "Why is Rossini addressing the *future?* Zounds! This animal now does nothing but talk too much about him in the *present*."

As for Rossini, he certainly could not suspect the degree to which, ten years later, when he would be no more, his prediction would be not only fulfilled but prodigiously exceeded.

Is it not a very extraordinary detail to remember about the composer of *Il Barbiere* and *Guillaume Tell*—that he had known, forty years apart, two vast geniuses, of whom the one, Beethoven, at the beginning of the century, revolutionized instrumental music—and of whom the other, Wagner, toward the end of the same era, was to revolutionize opera—while during that interval of waiting between *Fidelio* and *Tannhäuser*, it devolved upon him, the Italian, to fascinate his contemporaries by the melodious charm of new forms, of which he was the brilliant initiator, and to add his undeniable portion of influence to the future destinies of the musical drama?

I said above that the two masters never met again.

After the failure of *Tannhäuser* at the Paris Opéra,* French and some German journals published at Wagner's expense new stories, again attributed to Rossini. Then some maladroit friends intervened—one asks with what aim?—to present the Italian Maestro's attitude to Wagner's eyes in a disadvantageous light. Neither more nor less, they

---

* *Tannhäuser* was sung in French at the Opéra on March 13, 18, and 24, 1861. Disturbances created at its second and third performances by members of the Jockey Club insured its withdrawal from the boards.

pictured him as a false good fellow. I tried to enlighten Wagner on this subject and to tell him the exact truth.[18]

Rossini, no less annoyed, charged Liszt,

[18] I insisted above all that he should decide—with the aim of ending the persistence of these false rumors—to publish *in extenso* the account of what had occurred during his interview with Rossini; of the truly sympathetic welcome of which he had been the object; of the subjects, so full of interest, which had been broached during the course of their conversation . . . , etc. He refused. "What good would it do?" he answered. "With regard to what concerns his art and the way he practiced it, Rossini told me nothing more than his works demonstrate. On the other hand, if I report the exposition of my theories as I sketched them for him, that repetition would be as brief as it would be useless to the public, they being divulged sufficiently by my writings. Then there remains my appreciation of the man. Here, I confess to you, I was very much surprised to discover—if only in the way he talked to me about Bach and Beethoven —how much his intellect, nourished far more than I had believed on German art, showed itself to be superior. He grew swiftly in my estimation. Historically, the moment for judging him still has not arrived. He is in too good health and is too much in view as he walks about, the length of the Champs-Elysées (I have heard from those who meet him, all the way from the place de la Concorde to the Barrière de l'Étoile), for it to be possible to assign to him now the place that he will occupy among the masters, his predecessors and contemporaries who now walk, and forever, in the Elysian Fields of the other world." Wagner persisted in this view; one can detect it in the obituary article that he devoted to Rossini in 1869 [actually, 1868]. There he held himself to a very summary account of the 1860 interview.

among others, to invite Wagner to call upon him again so that he might furnish indisputable proofs of his entire innocence. Wagner declined that invitation, giving as his pretext that these pullulating tales would only increase from the moment when the press learned that he had called upon Rossini again; that these men had not as yet, in this regard, done anything but overlard their tittle-tattle with *Pater, peccavi;* that all this put him in a false position . . . that, furthermore, he kept himself from discussing Rossini further, never having veered away from the impression of profound sympathy for the nobility of his character which he [Wagner] had had since the first visit that he [Wagner] had paid him . . .

That was the end of the matter. He remained obdurate, though I unsuccessfully renewed a final invitation from Rossini, when he charged me with returning to Wagner's house the score of the "Gra-ner" Mass which Liszt had lent to the Maestro.

I believe that the real reason for Wagner's refusal lay rather in his conviction that undertaking a second interview with the Italian master would profit him little. The purpose that he had proposed to himself when soliciting the first interview had, as I have explained, been achieved. He desired nothing further.

The two masters, then, never saw one another again; but I can certify that whenever Rossini's name came from Wagner's lips or pen, the latter never departed from the deference and profound esteem that he had conceived for him. It was the same with Rossini, who later on often asked me about what success Wagner's operas were meeting with in Germany, and regarding which he often charged me with transmitting to the latter his congratulations and remembrances.

An Evening at Rossini's
in Beau-Sejour
(Passy) 1858*

---

* The publication date of this pamphlet often is given as
1858, the date of the meeting it describes. But Michotte's
mention in it of *Aida* "and its successors" among Verdi's
operas makes certain that it was written later than 1893, as
the *première* of *Falstaff*, the second—and last—"successor"
to *Aida* occurred in that year.

[PASSY 1858]

Rossini's reputation for wit is universal. How has his public reputation not been abused—in the past, and even now—by thoughtless attribution to him of quantities of nonsense, of vacuous quips, of tasteless and sometimes malicious remarks having nothing whatever in common with the refined sallies, the humorous repartee, the mischievous mots of which the composer of *Il Barbiere* was prodigal? By himself, he had more wit than the multitude of anonymous people who labored to assign their own jokes to him.

When, feeling well and surrounded by his preferred friends, he found himself in his chosen milieu, his conversation was of an incomparable

93

allure. What an abundance of memories, what a profusion of original ideas, of curious *aperçus*—not to mention the vivacity of his replies, his high-toned raillery, his unpredictableness—the words happily hit upon—the real pleasure in the charm of a picturesque way of speaking which was absolutely personal with him! [1]

In the following narrative—extracted from numerous notes that I have kept of intimate conversations—I have held to the purpose of integral transcription, of showing the reader a Rossini painted from life under circumstances in which, thanks to the presence of Alboni,* the Maestro improvised for us a detailed lecture on the principles followed in Italy in his time for teaching the great art of *bel canto* to the celebrated virtuosos of that era.

It was in Passy on a soft spring evening; Rossini [and Mme Rossini] had gathered around the

---

[1] He handled the French language perfectly, with the ease of a born Parisian. Furthermore, his second wife, Olympe Pélissier, was a Parisienne.

* Marietta Alboni (1823–1894) was one of the foremost contraltos of the 1840's, '50's, '60's, and '70's. An intimate friend of Rossini for some thirty years, she joined Adelina Patti in singing the *Quis est homo* from the *Stabat Mater* at his funeral in Paris on November 21, 1868. Her vocal range was extraordinary: it extended up from the G below the treble clef to the C above it; she sang soprano as well as contralto and mezzo-soprano roles.

table Mme Alboni, Prince Poniatowski,[2] Heugel,[3] Azévedo,[4] Scudo,[5] and the writer of this account.

We were taking coffee in the garden.

As was his habit after the evening meal, the Maestro lighted a cigar.

When taking it from a small box intended especially for that purpose, he said to Prince Poniatowski: "I don't offer you one of these cigars. They are so weak—the only ones, furthermore, that I can bear—that if were to give them to a corporal or, above all, to a sapper, they would both decamp *presto* rather than put themselves in a position of having to exhale such bland puffs."

This pleasant remark was a good omen, presaging mental treats of uncommon flavor for the rest of the evening.

He had spoken little during dinner, as usual, chewing having become a laborious process for him

---

[2] Senator, composer, creator of the opera *Pierre de Médicis*. [Prince Josef Poniatowski (1816–1873), a great-grandson of Stanislas II Augustus, King of Poland, was an operatic composer of some distinction and a long-time friend of Rossini.]

[3] The renowned publisher in the rue Vivienne. [Jacques-Léopold Heugel (1811–1883) took over the Meissonier music-publishing firm in 1812, changing its name to Heugel et Cie., as which it was active until 1940.]

[4] Music critic of *L'Opinion nationale*. [See translator's footnote, page 85.]

[5] Art critic of *La Revue des Deux-Mondes*. [Pierre Scudo (1806–1864), an opera singer turned journalist, was a leading reactionary music critic and a devoted Rossinian.]

after the disappearance of almost all of his teeth.[6]

We chatted on about this and that—about the news of the day . . . and precisely about Tamberlick's performances at the Théâtre-Italien. "On

---

[6] The time when the composer Carafa, a childhood friend, promised to have a set of false teeth made for him, citing himself as an example of their use. "Oh, you!" Rossini replied, "in your position as a professor of harmony, you have become familiar with substitutions with or without *appoggiature*, but I, I don't worry over them at all. As for my jaw, and how much of it is reflected in my music, I make fun of the others; furthermore, I don't like the *ut dièzes* [C-sharps].[1]

CARAFA: "The C-sharps?"

ROSSINI: "Look, when one is in the hands of dentists—those virtuosos of the gums—their *notes*—and I judge them from the metallic sounds that I hear emerging from my wife's purse [*bourse*], always are C-sharps."

[1] An allusion to the famous chest-tone C-sharp with which [Enrico] Tamberlik [the renowned tenor (1820–1889)] just then was attracting all Paris to the Théâtre-Italien in [Rossini's] *Otello*.

Rossini had a predilection for puns, particularly for those based on an allusion to musical terms. Example: one day he found [Luigi] Cherubini [(1760–1842), the distinguished composer and director of the Paris Conservatoire] in bed and complaining loudly of a *point de côté* [pain in the side]. "What nonsense!" Rossini exclaimed. "How nonsense?" the exasperated Cherubini replied. "Look, my physician, who just left here, is an ass and I, who am howling with pain, am a blockhead!" "Precisely, that's what I think. You, *you* can never have anything but a *contrepoint de côté* [counter-pain in the side, a pun on counterpoint]."

At these words, Cherubini was convulsed, not with pain, but with laughter.

that subject, Heugel," Rossini said. "I read in your *Ménéstrel* [*sic*] that at the performance of *Otello* the day before yesterday, after the explosion of the famous C-sharp, the audience seemed *transported* . . . *transported*, I suppose, by that excruciating shout, to an operating session in the maternity hospital. Oh, the ninnies!

"[Gilbert-Louis] Duprez * was the first one to think of chafing the Parisians' ears by disgorging in *Guillaume Tell* that chest-tone C of which I had never dreamed. [Adolphe] Nourrit ** had been satisfied with a head-tone C, which was what was required. Then, during my stay in Paris in 1837, *** just after Duprez's resounding debut in *Guillaume Tell*, the impetuous tenor came to see

* Duprez (1806–1896) made his Paris debut as Arnold in *Guillaume Tell* on April 17, 1837, and singlehandedly restored that opera to popularity, largely because of his unexampled chest-tone high C (he sang up to E in falsetto).

** Nourrit (1802–1839), who succeeded his father, Louis Nourrit, as leading tenor of the Paris Opéra, created four Rossinian roles: Néoclès in *Le Siège de Corinthe* (1826), Amenophis in *Moïse et Pharaon* (1827), Comte Ory in the opera of that name (1828), and Arnold in *Guillaume Tell* (1829), this last a part somewhat too high-lying and otherwise too difficult for him. He committed suicide at Naples when the censors there forbade the performance of *Poliuto*, an opera by Donizetti, who had designed its name role for him.

*** Rossini was not in Paris in 1837. His first visit to Paris after Duprez's sensational debut there in 1837 occurred in 1843—when the meeting with Duprez could have taken place.

me to invite me to hear him at the Opéra. "You come to see me instead," I told him. "You will produce your C for me alone, and I'll be more than flattered." I was staying with my friend [Eugène] Troupenas.* Duprez hastened to come. With Troupenas present, he sang for me—magnificently, I must admit—several fragments of my opera. At the approach of the *'Suivez-moi,'* ** I experienced the kind of anxious discomfort that some people feel when they know that a cannon is about to be shot off. Finally, he burst forth with the C! Zounds, what an uproar! I rose from the piano and rushed to a virtrine filled with very delicate Venetian glass which decorated Troupenas's salon. 'Nothing broken,' I exclaimed, 'That's wonderful!'

"Duprez appeared enchanted by my remark, which he took for a compliment in my style. 'Well, then, Maître, tell me sincerely, does my C please you?' 'Very sincerely, what pleases me most about your C is that it is over, and that I am no longer in danger of hearing it. I don't like unnatural effects. It strikes my Italian ear as having a strident timbre, like a capon squawking as its throat is slit. You are a

---

* Troupenas (1799–1850), a mathematician and intense music lover, began to publish music after inheriting a small fortune. He was a close friend of Rossini and the publisher of *Le Siège de Corinthe, Moïse et Pharaon, Le Comte Ory, Guillaume Tell,* and the *Stabat Mater.*
** In Arnold's *"Amis, amis."*

very great artist, a true new creator of the role of Arnold. Why in the devil abase your talent by using that humbug?' 'Because,' Duprez answered, 'Opéra subscribers are accustomed to it now; that C is my great success . . .' 'Well, would you like an even greater success? Unload them two at a time.'

"Now comes Tamberlick. That jokester, wanting ardently to demolish Duprez's C, has invented the chest-tone C-sharp and loaded it onto me. In the finale of my *Otello* there is, in fact, an A that I emphasized. I thought that it, by itself, launched with full lungs, would be ferocious enough to satisfy the *amour-propre* of tenors for all time. But look at Tamberlick, who has transformed it into C-sharp, and all the snobs are delirious! Last week, he asked to come to see me. I received him. But, fearing a second, aggravated edition of the Duprez adventure, I cautioned Tamberlick please, when he came to see me, to deposit his C-sharp on the hall tree and pick it up again, guaranteed intact, when he left."

A great success for the amazing story of those celebrated C's, which the Maestro told calmly and with few gestures, in a manner brought on by age, but without the imprint of the years having affected his mental vivacity, more comical and more mischievous than ever.

When the conversation had turned more general, Alboni interrupted it by asking us if we knew "*L'Amour à Pekin*," * one of the Maestro's recent compositions, which she had read through some days earlier.

Nothing more was needed to set tinder to the powder. We all asked for "*L'Amour à Pekin*."

"Oh!" Rossini said. "It's a humbug."

* "*L'Amour à Pekin—Petite Mélodie sur la gamme chinoise*" is one of the *Péchés de vieillesse*; it appears in the *Album de morceaux réservés*, of which it is number 5; it has been recorded; it was published in *Quaderni Rossiniani*, V (Pesaro, 1956).

Nevertheless, the Maestro rose and led us into the salon without having to be begged excessively.

Sitting down at the piano and opening the manuscript: "I assure you," he repeated, "that it's nothing but a hoax on the notes of the Chinese scale, which is made up entirely of a series of tones without semitones.

and descending:

Needless to insist upon how Alboni, with her sumptuous voice, did justice to the piece.

I must confess, however, that the broad rhythm and the vocal qualities that mark the piece do not compensate for its lack of inspiration, which was hindered by the suppression of the semitones, the non-use of which dulls the expressive effect and is of a nature to engender monotony. Only details in the accompaniment and, above all, the succession of chords underlining the notes of the descending scale in the peroration, surprise by their harmonization, as piquant as it is unexpected.

The title *"L'Amour à Pekin"* provoked, in

that intimate circle, some very droll comments. "Well, what can one do?" Rossini replied in his bantering tone. "Whether it's in *Pé-Kin* or whether it's in *Kin*-Campoix,* love proceeds as loves always do, sharps in the prelude, flats in the coda."

Then Alboni sang *"L'Orpheline du Tyrol,"* ** another of the maestro's recently hatched works. This really charming one was heard later during the soirées in the Chaussée d'Antin (Rossini's winter residence in Paris).

Because things were proceeding so well, Prince Poniatowski—and how right he was!—asked Alboni to sing the famous aria from *Semiramide*: *"Ah! quel giorno,"* *** one of the eminent singer's triumphs.

"Va bene!" she exclaimed, running toward

---

* *"Kin*-Campoix" is pronounced exactly like Quincampoix, the name of a Paris street. A rough equivalent would be "Whether it's in Walla-Walla or Wall Street . . ."

** *"L'Orpheline du Tyrol"* is another of the *Péchés de vieillesse;* it appears in the *Album français,* of which it is number 11; it was published in *Quaderni Rossiniani,* V (Pesaro, 1956).

*** Arsace's *scena* (Act I, Scene 5) begins with the recitative *"Eccomi alfine in Babilonia,"* continues with the cavatina *"Ah! quel giorno ognor rammento,"* and culminates in the florid cabaletta *"Oh! come da quel dì tutto, tutto per me cangiò."* Alboni was a foremost performer of the role of Arsace, which she often sang opposite Giulia Grisi.

Rossini, who had not risen from the piano. *"Benissime* for you, I'm sure," he told her, "but if you think that I can remember that old mummy dating from 1823 . . . the cavatina perhaps—but the rest . . . and the recitative?"

Astonishingly, the Maestro did not have copies of any of his early works in his home, not one of his forty operatic scores, whether in manuscript or as published.

When someone expressed astonishment over that fact, he answered: "And I, do you think that I'd be less astonished if you were to tell me that you had preserved, you, your old matchboxes and worn slippers?"

After a moment of reflection, the Maestro finally gave in to our insistence: "All right, so be it," he said to Alboni. "Let's attempt it. But all that I have retained of the recitative is the first words: *"Ecco mi al fine in Babilonia."* For the rest, you prompt me. So much the worse if I get mixed up. The devil will be to get to the cavatina without embarrassment. From that point on, I really hope to be able to save the rest."

Needless to say, everything went well.

How describe the unforgettable emotion that seized upon us while we were listening, perhaps for the last time, to that celebrated aria in all its splendid pomp and as only Alboni still had the style to

interpret it, that model of vocal magnificence of
which Garcia * said that "if all the vocal pieces of
the Italian masters were to be destroyed, that aria
would by itself suffice for reconstituting the entire
art of *bel canto*"?

After the disappearance of the great virtuosos:
the Nozzaris, Gallis, Davides, Rubinis,** and—
among the female singers—the Colbrans, Pastas,
Sontags, Pisaronis,*** and, most marvelous of them

---

* This could refer to either Manuel del Popolo Vicente
Garcia (1775–1832), renowned tenor (the first Almaviva in
Il Barbiere di Siviglia), composer, and singing teacher, or
his son Manuel Patricio (1805–1906), one of the greatest of
singing teachers.

** Andrea Nozzari (1775–1832), a tenor, created roles in
nine of Rossini's operas. Filippo Galli (1783–1853), originally a tenor, became a notable *basso cantante* and created
roles in eight of Rossini's operas and in Donizetti's *Anna
Bolena*. Giacomo David(e) (1750–1830) was a leading tenor
of the eighteenth century. His son Giovanni (1790–1864)
was equally renowned in the nineteenth; he created roles in
six of Rossini's operas. Giovanni Battista Rubini (1795–1854),
regarded by many of his contemporaries as the finest tenor
of his time, was noted for his assumption of many Rossinian
and Donizettian roles.

*** Isabella Colbran (1786–1845) was Rossini's first wife;
he shaped leading parts in ten of his Neapolitan operas for
her. Giuditta Pasta (1799–1865), a foremost soprano of her
time, appeared in the *première* of only one Rossinian opera
(*Il Viaggio a Reims*, 1825), but sang with enormous success
in most of the outstanding operas available to her. Henriette
Sontag (1806–1854), a soprano, created the title role in
Weber's *Euryanthe* and sang in the first performances of
Beethoven's *Missa solemnis* and Ninth Symphony; she also

all, the genius-gifted Malibran *—in a word, after that admirable school of which Alboni remains the final glory, our ears were not used to that masterly diction, to such solid *sostenuto* in that largo, with its lapidary structure "*Ah! quel giorno*," which ten cellos (Prince Poniatowski's remark was just) could not equal! I should add the impression made by the feverish vigor of the allegro: "*Oh! come da quel dì*," in which, despite the fast tempo of the writing and the multiplicity of notes, not one of them was slighted, not one but emerged without shock, without violence, in its full sonorous value!

When, borne away with admiration, we surrounded the great artist, Rossini became very animated and departed this time from the feigned or real indifference that he ordinarily displayed when, as he said, people made him "unpack one of his old things"—Rossini affectionately embraced his Marietta (he had known Alboni as a child at the Bologna Liceo and had been particularly involved

excelled in Italian opera. Benedetta Rosmunda Pisaroni (1793–1872), a contralto, created roles in three of Rossini's operas.

* Maria Malibran (1808–1836), daughter of Manuel del Popolo Vicente García, sister of Pauline Viardot-García and Manuel Patricio García, was one of the two or three greatest operatic singers of her era. She sang in several Rossini operas with clamorous success.

in her vocal education). Then he sighed: *"Ahi noi! perduto il bel canto della patria!* [Alas for us!—our homeland's *bel canto* is lost!]."

Then he added: "At present, with our so-called singers, *bel canto* is produced with a convulsive thrusting of the lips, from which there emerges, particularly with tenor-baritones, a tremolo that closely resembles the buzzing produced in my ears by the way the floor shakes at the approach of my brewer's chariot; whereas tenors and prime donne allow themselves—the former, vociferations, the latter, garglings [*gargouillades*], and these have in relation to REAL *vocalizations* and *roulades* nothing but the consonance of the rhymes."

Alboni added: "And the portamentos, which you haven't mentioned."

"Ah, yes! that plague," Rossini replied. "It had little place in my time. It happened, however, that the sorts of braying produced from top to bottom and the trumpetings loosed from bottom to top succeeded in astonishing the public's ears sometimes. Well, I advised the virtuosos of those eccentric mouthings to go and ask for bravos and recalls from the denizens of zoölogical gardens."

(We may presume that at the time these blows with the paw, as penetrating as they were

intelligently conceived, referred to the interpreters
of the operas—then much in vogue—of Verdi, the
vocal form of which, the antipodes of the Rossinian
style, had brought into style effects that were
incorrect, harsh, and violent; and which con-

tributed brutally to hastening the rapid decay of
the Italian school of *bel canto*. In that connection,
Rossini was credited with a mot that the press hastened to spread; he was supposed to have said of
Verdi: "He is a musician who wears a helmet." But
the report was inexact; here is the truth. After

reading one of Verdi's scores, the Maestro exclaimed: "If the name of the composer had been kept hidden from me, I should have wagered that he could only be an artillery colonel.") (I should add that at that time Verdi still had not written the scores of *Aida* and its successors.)

"Maestro," we demanded, "do you really believe that *bel canto* is irretrievably lost?"

"Absolutely," he answered sharply. "And at the beginning, let us understand what we mean by the term. Here, *bel canto* generally is confused with *fioriture*. That is a mistake. *Bel canto* is made up of three elements:

"1. The instrument—the voice—the *Stradivarius*, if you like;

"2. Technique—that is to say, the means of using it;

"3. *Style*, the ingredients of which are taste and feeling.

"Let's speak first of the voice, the instrument to be formed. Nature, alas, never creates all parts of a voice perfectly, any more than a pine tree gives birth to a *Stradivarius*. Just as an instrument maker must construct a Stradivarius, so it behooves a future singer to fabricate the instrument he counts upon using. And how long and arduous a labor that is!

"Among my compatriots, that job formerly was facilitated; in view of nature's refusal to comply, they made *castrati*. The method, to be sure, was heroic, but the results were wonderful. In my youth it was my good fortune still to be able to hear some of those fellows.

"I have never forgotten them. The purity, the miraculous flexibility of those voices and, above all, their profoundly penetrating accent—all that moved and fascinated me more than I can tell you. I should add that I myself wrote a role for one of them, one of the last but not of the least—Velluti.* That was in my opera *Aureliano in Palmira*, which was given in Milan in 1813.

"Would you believe, parenthetically, that I came within a hair's breadth of belonging to that famous corporation—let us, rather, say decorporation. As a child, I had a very pretty voice, and my parents used it to have me earn a few paoli by singing in churches. One uncle of mine, my mother's brother, a barber by trade,** had convinced my father of the opportunity that he had glimpsed if the breaking of my voice should not be

---

* Giovanni Battista (Giambattista) Vellutti (1780–1861) was a renowned soprano *castrato;* he was greatly admired in Vienna and London.
** Rossini's maternal uncle Francesco Maria Guidarini.

allowed to compromise an organ which—poor as we were, and I having shown *some* disposition toward music—could have become an assured future source of income for us all. Most of the *castrati*, and particularly those dedicated to a theatrical career, in fact lived in opulence. My brave mother would not consent at any price."

"And you, Maestro, the chief interested party?" Scudo asked.

"Oh! me," Rossini answered, "all that I can tell you is that I was very proud of my voice . . . And as for any descendants that I might leave . . ."

Mme Rossini interrupted: "Little you cared! Now is the moment for making one of your quips."

"Well, then, let's have no half-truths," the Maestro replied. " 'Little' is too much. I didn't care at all."

Then, after giving some details of the extraordinary virtuosity of the *castrati*, the Maestro went on in this way:

"Ah, yes, in those days the formation of the voice, the instrument, was an ungrateful labor.

"It began with work exclusively on the pure and simple emission of sound. Homogeneity of timbre, equalization of the registers—that was the basis of the apprenticeship upon which all later study was based. That practical instruction filled up at least three years of exercises.

"When I went back to stay in Bologna after abandoning my theatrical career, I was entirely

taken up with the teaching of singing at the Liceo. I just mentioned homogeneity of timbre, equalization of the registers. Here, for example, is a model of the exercises that I prescribed, thanks to which I obtained astonishing results. It is simple, and the pupil himself, given a good ear, came to be able to correct himself." Then, sitting down at the piano, the Maestro struck the following notes:

"After which the same exercise was continued through ascending semitones C-C-sharp, D-D-sharp, E, etc., to the limit of the voice's tessitura, variable according to age and to the progress of the martyr or *victim*," Rossini said, exchanging a smile with his illustrious former pupil Alboni.

"Without that first discipline, aimed at developing equality of timbre over the whole range of the organ, a voice, no matter how richly endowed by nature it may be, always will remain completely defective. Isn't that the case, what's more, with the brain, the most generous innate capacities of which demand long, studious effort if they are to acquire their full value?"

Then, continuing his demonstration: "Upon certain pupils, whose emission was functionally faulty, often as the result of a not very appropriate development of the voice, the teacher imposed special gymnastics of guttural contractions that the patient, I must say, had to practice without emitting the tiniest sound; that purely aphonic gymnastic could go on for months and months.

"When the voice finally had acquired the desired suppleness and equality—that is to say, when the future singer was in possession of his Stradivarius—only then did he begin to learn *the way to use* it! THE TECHNIQUE, which included placement, the holding of sound, and all the exercises in virtuosity: *vocalises, gruppetti,* trills, etc."

Alboni interrupted. "For three years, my teacher kept me at a single page, which I still have, and which includes by itself all the types of scholastic exercises for holding, agility, etc."

"And which taught you," Rossini added, "to construct the sound somewhat differently from today's practice; for now the would-be singers are, we must agree, peculiar apostles. Whereas a long apprenticeship is necessary in order to play the clarinet, an instrument that is *already made,* these singers, vainly confident about an instrument that has not yet been made at all—that is, a worn, unequal, badly placed voice—approach the public without wincing, all the while not knowing how to tame a note without repeating it in some way, nor how to let it die out naturally without a glottal stroke with the quality of an aborted hiccough.

"And there you have the miscarriages over which present-day snobbism swoons! *Miseria!*

"If I have spoken only of male singers," the Maestro added with a sly air, "don't think that I shall plait wreathes for the ladies. On the contrary!"

Then he went on: "After that, the work with the vowels began. Here is what that consisted of: the placement of the sounds and the *vocalises* were practiced from the first on the vowels, one at a time, a, e, i, o, u; then all five of them were produced alternatively on the same held tone or the same figure.

"For example:

"This system was practiced on all the sustained tones and through all the exercises, which were complicated to infinity.

"The aim was to reach the point at which, as much as possible, the sound would not vary in timbre or intensity in spite of movements of the tongue and displacements of the lips caused by the succession of vowels, sometimes open, sometimes closed. In that way, one obtained o's that did not seem to have come from a megaphone, e's that did not resemble the noise of a rattle, and i's that were not mixed *à la vinaigrette.** That was one of the subtlest parts of the teaching.

"The study of the vowels was followed by that of the diphthongs, consonants, articulation, breathing, etc. Special attention was paid, above all, to the sound created with the help of the roof of the mouth. In fact, it is the transmitter *par excellence* of beautiful sounds. And in that regard one must agree that the Italian language really seems privileged to favor the evolution of *bel canto. Amâre . . . bêllo . . .* Those *mâ*s and *bêll*s, placed in the roof of the mouth and sounded thus—isn't that already a sort of music?

"A student showing any tendency to roll his

---

* It should be kept in mind that in both Italian and French the vowel *e* has something the sound of the English interjection *eh*, *i* that of the long English *e* (as in *see*).

r's, to lisp, to quaver, or to spice his emission with a dash of the guttural would have been singled out as a dangerous being liable to banishment if he remained impervious to correction. As for such as trumpeted through their noses, the teacher ordinarily advised them to enroll in a fanfare corps." [7]

[7] He sometimes gave the most laughable characterizations of some of these defects:

To a person who sang a cavatina for him in an obstinately guttural manner: "There's a cavatina," he said, "that seems to be coming out of a cave. You must know that caves are said to produce good mushrooms? Frankly, I'd have preferred a plate of that sort."

A friend had asked him to agree to hear a young tenor; unhappily, the man rolled his r's terribly. Suddenly the Maestro, who was at the piano, stopped playing, turned aside, and said: "Where, then did you get the habit of winding your watch while singing?"

A baritone much in favor with the public had sought the privilege of singing for the Maestro. He had talent; but—a fault commoner than you might believe—he made the succeeding word wait more or less upon the note. "A beautiful voice," Rossini said, "but you have a case of syllabic constipation. You must take care of that."

A not unpicturesque remark about an obese lady singer whose mouth had all but vanished in an incredible mass of fat. The unfortunate woman stammered outrageously as a result of that superabundant generosity on nature's part. "That's what you might call singing *properly*," Rossini said. "Each note creates the effect of having escaped from a tub of lard."

One day he was asked by his barber to examine the man's son, who was reputed to possess an unparalleled voice. In fact, it was a thunderous organ of rare species. Unhappily, nature also had given the fellow a roughness that the Mae-

"The third phase of the training consisted of putting into practice as a whole everything that had been studied in detail over a period of not less than five years for girls, seven for men. Then, at the end of a final year, the teacher could say proudly to that student—who had scarcely tried out a cavatina in class: 'Go now, get on with you. You can sing whatever you wish.'

"That is the truth. He was capable of singing anything. And nevertheless, something remained for him to learn; that something without which the most accomplished virtuosity, even when it bears the imprimatur of many awards won in the Liceo, still remains in some way comparable to an or-

---

stro compared to a steel file. "Under these circumstances," he said, "that is an irremediable vice. But don't take it too hard. Your son has many resources for becoming a commander of zouaves, a barricade chief, an animal tamer—or, above all, the times being what they are, a first-prize winner at the Conservatoire."

A friend who was a good musician wrote him from Dieppe: "There is a young girl here who has an admirable voice. She has only one dream, which is for you to hear her. If you agree, she will leave for Paris at once, accompanied by her mother. I believe that she has a fortune in her throat." The Maestro responded: "Given that that's the way it is, dissuade these ladies from making the trip to Paris. But persuade them to go to a surgeon as soon as possible so that he can extract *prestissimo* from that phenomenal throat the fortune that it contains. Can one ever be certain of the future? A bird in the hand is worth two in the bush!"

And so on without end.

ganism full of latent life but awaiting a ray of warm sunlight to transform itself into movement, strength, magnificence, and seductiveness.

"That warm ray—it is *style*. Style is traditions, and the secrets of those traditions could be surprised by the young novice only among great singers, the perfect models consecrated by fame.

"Those traditions, on the other hand, elude scholastic instruction. Only the *performing model*, taken from life, can inculcate and transmit them. So that if those who possess the great, true traditions disappear without leaving disciples on their level, their art vanishes, dies. *De profundis!* . . . In my time, there were numerous incomparable virtuosos in whose presence the new adepts could initiate themselves into taste, elegance, the judicious use of all the vocal effects—into *style*, that is.

"As for the qualities of expression, feeling, grace, charm, stage insight: that is an affair of the individual temperament.

"Let's finish, then: today there is no such school, there are neither models nor interpreters, for which reason not a single voice of the new generation is capable of rendering in *bel canto* the aria 'Casta Diva' [8] or 'Pria che spunti'; [9] or any

---

[8] From Bellini's *Norma*.
[9] From Cimarosa's *Il Matrimonio segreto*.

other you like—how can you imagine that it is possible to resuscitate what is dead, what is less than a mummy?

"What genius, be he more perspicacious than a Champollion,* could succeed in reconstituting that which has no tradition but oral tradition—let us rather say vocal tradition? And then, a parallel phenomenon will suggest itself: whence and by what miracle will disciples appear who, in our times, will consent to submit to the long, severe regimen that I just detailed?

"The railroads, a devilish invention, have unsettled everything—not to mention the formidable currents of international air, the permanent breathing of which, as they blow through those multiple tunnels of Hell, finally will give all humanity a cold—has instilled into the present generation the need to get things done quickly, the fever to arrive. The theaters pullulate; the impresarios, who are legion, carve arrows out of any kind of wood. And behold! . . . Here, for example, my concierge's daughter. She is eighteen, and she aspires to learn singing so as to go into the theater. One won't ever be able to remove from her head the idea that at the end of one year she will be arch-capable of making a debut in *Les Hugue-*

---

* Jean-François Champollion (1790–1832) worked out, from study of the Rosetta stone, the secret of deciphering Egyptian hieroglyphics.

nots!" * With his mischievous air, Rossini added: "Who would dare assert that she won't become a celebrity as a result, a Patti,** a star to be cited as a model of perfection? At the present time, that's not so difficult!"

"Speaking of Patti, whose name you just mentioned," Heugel interrupted, "what, dear Maître, is your final opinion of her talent?"

"My opinion is that she is charming and that I love her very much."

"And then? . . ."

"And then . . . that fate has been very gallant toward her in protecting her from the danger of being contemporary with, for example, Sontag . . . not to cite others."

"Which means," Azevedo answered, "that today, lacking thrushes, we must content ourselves with blackbirds."

Rossini said nothing more. A significant pause.

"Well," we said, "with you, Maestro, it is necessary, then, to repeat in chorus: '*De profundis il bel canto?*'"

"Certainly," Rossini added, "one still encoun-

---

* Opera by Giacomo Meyerbeer.
** Adelina Patti (1843–1919), one of the most agile and popular of operatic sopranos and a friend of Rossini. She made her official debut, as Lucia di Lammermoor, in New York on November 24, 1859, when only sixteen.

ters singers who are thoroughbreds, really great singers who apply the highest qualities of dramatic expression, of theatrical understanding, to inter-preting—supposing that their imperfect vocal tech-niques will still permit it—the roles that were made to be sung by the masters who in their time wrote for *the voice that sings*. As for the composers who write for *the voice that does not sing*, would you call their interpreters singers?

"That would be like calling laborers the no-mads who cross the desert sand trying to collect a few blades of grass there. But, truly, such great singers as Nozzari, Davide, Garcia, Rubini . . . and admirable ladies like Marcolini,* Colbran, Pasta, Sontag, and Malibran—I cite only a few names among the vanished glories representing the divine art of song at perfection—they will appear no more . . . unless it should be the aforementioned daughter of my concierge!"

Amid the laughter evoked by this last sally:

"And among the elite lady singers whom you have just enumerated, Maestro, which—we ask you—do you judge to have been the greatest?"

"The greatest was *Colbran*, who became my first wife, but the *unique* was *Malibran*. Ah! that

---

* Maria Marcolini (1780–?), a contralto, was especially noted for her comic roles. She created parts in five of Rossini's operas.

marvelous creature! She surpassed all her imitators by her truly disconcerting musical genius, and all the women I have ever known by the superiority of her intelligence, the variety of her knowledge,

and her flashing temperament, of which it is impossible to give any idea. Knowing the most diverse languages, she sang in Spanish (her native tongue), Italian, French, German, and after eight days of study, she sang *Fidelio* in English in London. She sketched, painted, embroidered, sometimes made her own costumes; above all, she wrote. Her letters are masterpieces of subtle intelligence, of verve, of good humor, and they display unparalleled originality of expression.

"In that connection, I'll tell you about an
event that, under Malibran's influence, later resulted in a very curious change in my habits. At the
time when I was composing, I refused to put my
foot inside the theater again to hear an opera once
the rehearsals were over. An exception, however;
but one I was forced to by contract. I had conducted the *première* of *Il Barbiere* at Rome. The
work fell flat. Coming out of the theater by a secret
door, I was recognized, unfortunately; an angry
mob, with raised fists, pursued me with such rage,
mixed with hisses, whoops, and even projectiles,
that I thought that the end of my existence had
come.

"You here, you have not the least notion of
the excesses of which the descendants of the gentle
Numa Pompilius * are capable when, gathered in a
theater to attend the *première* of a new work, they
decide that they are not getting their money's
worth. They inflict upon the unhappy author the
severest punishment, for which one can only pity
him. Me, I had been punished by the ruining of a
handsome new jacket with gold buttons which I
had had made for me at the expense of my poor

---

* A legendary Sabine king of Rome (715–673 B.C.).

purse so that I might look decent on the conductor's podium. That unhappy jacket, which was of a hazel color, was ruined by the filth with which it had been covered during the uproar. I asked the servant at my hotel to accept it as it was—naturally, after I had removed the gold buttons, which were worth thirty francs."

"A relic which, if it could be found again," Prince Poniatowski exclaimed, "would not, in its pacific way, be out of place alongside the terrible gray cloak." *

"However, Maestro, one must add," Azevedo said, "that you were vindicated triumphantly the next day, when the same Romans, coming from the second performance of *Il Barbiere,* arrived in a crowd to give you an ovation."

"Stop!" Rossini said. "You are reminding me of the greatest fright that I ever felt in my life. I was peacefully sleeping when I was awakened suddenly by a deafening uproar in the street, accompanied by a bright glow of torches which I saw approaching the hotel as soon as I got up. Still half asleep, and recalling the scene of the preceding night, I thought that they were coming to set fire to the building, and so I took the precaution of going to a stable at the back of the courtyard. But behold, after a few instants I hear García calling me at the

---

* Apparently a reference to Napoleon's *"terrible capote gris."*

top of his voice. He finally found me. 'Get a move on you; come now; hear those shouts of *bravo, bravissimo Figaro*. An unprecedented success. The street is full of people; they want to see you.' 'Tell them,' I answered—still having at heart the fact that my new jacket had gone to the devil, 'that I f . . . them, their bravos, and all the rest. I'm not coming out of here.' I don't know how poor García presented my refusal to that turbulent crowd—in fact, he was struck in the eye by an orange, tumefied traces of which formed a black circle visible for several days. Meanwhile, the uproar in the street increased more and more . . . The proprietor of the hotel arrived in turn, breathless: 'If you don't come out, they'll set fire to my building; now they're breaking windows . . .' 'That's your affair,' I told him, 'you have only to avoid standing behind your windows . . . Me, I'm staying where I am.' Finally I heard panes of glass crashing. Then, war-weary, the crowd finally dispersed. I left my refuge and went back to bed. Unhappily, the brigands had defenestrated two windows facing the bed. It was January.* I should be lying if I told you that the icy air coming into my room gave me a delicious night!

"The next morning, the hotel keeper came to tell me that the loss he had suffered in fifteen bro-

* The date was actually February 22, 1816.

ken windows was entirely a result of my stubbornness, and that he had the right to put the costs on my bill, but that he wouldn't do anything if I would agree to get out of his hotel within twenty-four hours. Entirely in accord with him about that very agreeable project, I installed myself in the diligence leaving for Naples the next day. All the interpreters of my *Barbiere*, hearing about my precipitous departure, came to bid me farewell. I was touched most by the visit of García, my incomparable *Almaviva*, accompanied by his eight-year-old daughter, the future Malibran! As soon as she came in, she bounded toward me and, dissolved in tears, clung to my neck, crying: 'Ah! if mama only had sent me to the theater last night!'

" 'And what would you have done?'

" 'Oh, while they were hissing your beautiful music, I should have shouted with all my strength: "You are all snakes; go back to the wild places and understand the music of the bears, the only sort that you deserve!" '

"She really would have been capable of doing just that," Rossini added, "for she was a little demon. Then she said to me: 'Don't be sad: listen: when I am grown up, I'll sing *Il Barbiere* everywhere, but (tapping her foot) never at *Rome*, even if the Pope on both knees begs me to.'

"When the visit was over, she was still throwing me from the door a quantity of kisses from her little hands, and she went away singing 'Una voce poco fa.' Would you believe that that *gamine*, after attending only a few rehearsals of *Il Barbiere*, had remembered nearly all of the pieces?"

The Maestro went back to his story: "I said then that once the rehearsals were over, it was my custom never to attend a performance of any of my operas. That surprises you? Frankly, what would have been the sense of my wasting my time in order to find out how I had written them?"

"It even seems," Scudo observed, "that you have never been to a single performance of *Guillaume Tell* at the Opéra."

"That is true. The singers came to rehearse at my place—I was living in the boulevard Montmartre, above the passage Jouffroy. After hearing two complete rehearsals in succession, though without the stage costumes, I had had enough. Until—and now I return to my subject—it was a question of performances with Malibran. That was something else. When she was to appear in *Semiramide*, *La Gazza ladra*, *Cenerentola*, *Il Barbiere*, above all in *Otello*, nothing could have kept me from going to hear her. The fact was that each time her creative genius inspired her in a stupefying, always different way with unexpected effects, both vocal and declamatory . . . Each time, too, she taught me how I could have done *better* than I had done."

The conversation continued merrily. Scudo,

who at the time was busy on a history of the Théâtre-Italien, said: "Maître, a few moments ago you
mentioned the names of admirable virtuosos who
graced the era of your youth. What comparison
would you make between them and their successors, the ones whose undeniable talent continues
today to maintain the glory of the Italian
schools—such as Mario, Gardoni, Zucchini, Badiali, Tamburini * . . . and, among the women,
Frezzolini, Grisi, Bosio, Borghi-Mamo,** etc?

---

* Mario, Cavaliere di Candia (1810–1883), a tenor, made
his operatic debut in Meyerbeer's *Robert le Diable* at the
Paris Opéra in 1838; he retired in 1867 after a very successful career; he married Giulia Grisi. Italo Gardoni
(1821–1882), a tenor, sang successfully from 1840 to about
1870; he created a role in Verdi's London opera, *I Masnadieri*. Giovanni Zucchini (1812–1892), a *buffo* baritone, was
a leading singer from about 1848 to 1884; he was particularly
admired in *Il Barbiere di Siviglia* and Donizetti's *Don
Pasquale*. Cesare Badiali (1810?–1865), a bass, made his operatic debut when very young; he sang to acclaim in operas by
Rossini, Donizetti, and Verdi; in 1842, he sang in Rossini's
Stabat Mater at Vienna under Donizetti's direction. Antonio Tamburini (1800–1876), a bass-baritone, was one of the
foremost operatic singers of his era; he created roles in
almost a dozen of Donizetti's operas (he was the first Mala-
testa in *Don Pasquale*).
    ** Erminia Frezzolini (1820–1884), a daughter of the
noted *basso buffo* Giuseppe Frezzolini and wife of the tenor
Antonio Poggi, became a much-appreciated operatic soprano; she created the role of Giselda in Verdi's *I Lombardi
alla prima crociata* (1843). Giulia Grisi, a niece of the
renowned contralto Giuseppina Grassini, a sister of the
mezzo-soprano Giuditta Grisi, and a cousin of the singer

"Naturally, I do not mention our Alboni or Lablache,* both of whom are unequaled."

"Certainly," Rossini replied, "their technical education was not subjected to the severe, long-applied principles of which I gave you a brief sketch; but some part of the good tradition has remained familiar to them. There are still stars of a beautiful grandeur. But it soon will be difficult to find among the reputations now in vogue, Faure ** excepted, newly emerged models worthy

Ernesta Grisi (Mme Théophile Gautier) and the great ballerina Carlotta Grisi, married as her second husband the tenor known as Mario. She shared the general repertoire of her foremost "rivals": Giuditta Pasta, Maria Malibran, and Henriette Sontag. Angiolina Bosio (1830–1859) made her debut at Milan in 1846 in Verdi's *I Due Foscari*. Becoming internationally famous as a soprano, she visited Havana, New York, Philadelphia, and Boston—and died in a carriage en route from Moscow to St. Petersburg. Adelaide Borghi-Mamo (1829–1901), a noted contralto (her daughter Erminia later became a noted soprano), was famed for her roles in operas by Rossini, Donizetti, and Verdi.

* Luigi Lablache (1794–1858), born in Naples of French parents, became the foremost *basso buffo* of his time and one of its leading *bassi cantanti*. He created roles in Bellini's *I Puritani di Scozia* (1835), Donizetti's *Marino Faliero* (1835) and (title role) *Don Pasquale* (1843), and (opposite Jenny Lind) Verdi's *I Masnadieri* (1847).

** Jean-Baptiste Faure (1830–1914), the foremost French bass-baritone of his time, created many roles, including Nelusko in Meyerbeer's *L'Africaine* (1865), Rodrigo in Verdi's *Don Carlos* (1867), and the title role in Ambroise Thomas's *Hamlet* (1868). He was a renowned Méphistophélès in Gounod's *Faust;* he is also remembered as the composer of the song "Les Rameaux."

of comparison to them. Alas! time, the obliterator, gradually will close in over these latter. After which, a few rare nebulae still, here and there . . . Then, no more . . . the final night."

"In the meantime"—it was the voice of Mme Rossini—"another sort of night had arrived, announced by the clock. It is ten o'clock."

"The canonical hour" (the Maestro's phrase for his invariable retiring time).

"Then, *messieurs*" [Mme Rossini said], "I shall take you all to the door. You must see that this evening you have subtly *emptied* my husband again. You are unbearable friends, examining magistrates; won't your interrogations ever come to an end?"

"Never! Madame . . . insatiable like treasure hunters!" Azevedo replied.

That was the final word.

Buona sera. To Alboni, who went up to embrace him: *"Buona sera, l'ultima diva del mio cuore* [Good night, final *diva* of my heart]."

That is a specimen of one of the numerous conversations in which, as we have just seen, having a place in which to enjoy himself when surrounded by a circle of intimate friends, the Maestro minced no words. During the gala soirées in the Chaussée d'Antin, on the other hand, where a crowd always gathered, he did not open his mouth.

Appendix

Eduard Hanslick's Visits to Rossini

in 1860 and 1867

Emil Naumann's Visit to Rossini

in 1867

SHORTLY after Wagner's call at Rossini's Paris home, the distinguished Viennese critic Eduard Hanslick (1825–1904), perhaps the leading anti-Wagnerian (he is caricatured in *Die Meistersinger von Nürnberg* as Sixtus Beckmesser), visited Rossini. In an article entitled "Musical Recollections of Paris (1860)," included in his *Aus dem Concert-Saal* (Vienna, 1897 edition), Hanslick wrote of Rossini:

"Great musical controversies and turning points, as for example *Zukunftsmusik* [the Wagner-Liszt "music of the future"], have no interest

beyond curiosity for the composer of *Il Barbiere*.
A year ago Rossini took the baths at Kissingen.
When he appeared in the pump room, the orchestra at once played selections from his operas. 'You
can scarcely imagine how boring that was for me. I
thanked the conductor and told him that I'd much
rather hear something that I didn't know, something by Richard Wagner, for example.' He then
heard the *Tannhäuser* March, which he quite liked,
and another piece that he could no longer recall;
that's all that he knew of Wagner. Rossini wanted
to know something about the story of *Lohengrin*.
After I had explained it as briefly and clearly as
possible, he exclaimed gaily in his funny accent:
'*Ah, je comprends! c'est un Garibaldi qui s'en va
aux nues!* [Ah, I see, it's a Garibaldi who's taken up
into the clouds].' Richard Wagner, who had visited the old gentleman recently, 'didn't seem at all
like a revolutionary'; anyone who knows that
dainty little man, that untiring and witty conversationalist, will gladly agree with that. Wagner, Rossini continued, introduced himself immediately
with the quieting assurance that he had not the
slightest intention of overthrowing existing music
as people said he had. 'Dear sir,' Rossini interrupts
him, 'that's of no importance at all; if your revolution succeeds, then you were absolutely right; if
you don't succeed, then, with or without revolu-

tion, you miscalculated.' Rossini did not want to
hear anything about a mischievous joke then circu-
lating in Paris which compared Wagner's music to
'fish sauce without fish'; I would have believed him
completely if he had not added in his droll, solemn
manner: '*Je ne dis jamais de telles choses* [I never
say such things].' Well, one knows so many and
such clever '*de telles choses*' by Rossini that his
inclination to irony is utterly beyond doubt. In that
vein, he is credited with having exclaimed recently,
after looking through a Berlioz score, 'How fortunate that this is not music!' "

More than seven years later, Hanslick wrote,
in one of his "Musical Letters from Paris" (July
18, 1867, in the 1897 Vienna edition of *Aus dem
Concert-Saal*), of a second call upon Rossini, who
by then was seventy-five years old. Suddenly Rossini had asked whether or not the Beethoven monu-
ment in Vienna had been completed. " 'I remember
Beethoven very well,' Rossini went on after a brief
pause, 'though it will soon be half a century. During my stay in Vienna, I hastened to seek him
out.'—'And, as [Anton Felix] Schindler * and
other biographers assure us, he didn't admit
you.'—'On the contrary,' Rossini corrected me, 'I

* Schindler (1795–1864) for a time served as Beethoven's
friendly secretary. His *Biographie Ludwig van Beethovens*
was published at Münster in 1840.

had asked the Italian poet Carpani, with whom I had visited Salieri earlier, to introduce me to Beethoven, who received us at once, and very politely. Of course, the visit didn't last very long, as conversation with Beethoven really was painful. He was hearing especially badly that day, and though I spoke as loudly as possible, he didn't understand me; furthermore, his lack of facility in Italian may have made the conversation even more difficult for him.' I confess that this information, the truth of which was corroborated by numerous details, pleased me like an unexpected gift. I always had been irritated by this incident in Beethoven's life, as well as by those musical Jacobins who had glorified the brutal German virtue of denying admittance to a Rossini. Well, the whole story was false.* Another example of the unconcern with which incorrect data are presented and repeated so that they can harden into historic truth at an incredible rate. And all that while it still would be so easy to obtain authentic enlightenment from living participants!"

About three months before Hanslick's 1867 visit to Rossini, Emil Naumann (1827–1888), Ger-

---

* This fictitious account of Beethoven's rudeness to Rossini nonetheless was repeated in several biographies of Beethoven, including that by Wilhelm Joseph von Wasielewski (*Beethoven*, 2 vols., 1888).

man composer and writer, had called on the elderly Italian. In his 1876 book *Italienische Tondichter, von Palestrina bis auf die Gegenwart,* Naumann wrote:

"Suddenly he [Rossini] interrupted himself with the words: '*A propos,* how is Monsieur Richard Wagner? Is he still the idol of Germany, or has the fever with which he infected your compatriots subsided? But, wait a moment—I am so thoughtless—perhaps you yourself are a Wagnerian, and if so perhaps you don't think that you and the other German are plagued by a fever, but rather that the one who is is I, the old man?' I assured him that he need not worry in that respect, my ideals being our great classical composers; nevertheless, I could not refrain from declaring that, Mendelssohn, Robert Schumann, and Meyerbeer now being dead, Richard Wagner was the most significant and independent talent among living German composers.—'Oh, in that respect, I completely agree with you,' Rossini exclaimed, 'and nothing could be farther from my mind than doubting the originality of the creator of *Lohengrin;* but occasionally the composer makes it very hard for us to find the beauties for which we are indebted to him amid the chaos of sounds that his operas contain. You will have experienced that yourself: *Monsieur Wagner a de beaux moments, mais de mauvais quart-d'heures!* [Monsieur Wagner has beautiful moments, but bad longueurs]! There is only one thing that I never understood and still cannot understand: how it is possible for a people that has produced a Mozart ever to begin to forget him because of a Wagner!' "

Index

Index

Bellini, Vincenzo, 118 *n*, 129 *n*
Berlioz, Louis-Hector, 133
Beyle, Henri ("Bombet," "Stendhal"), 41 *n*
Biographie Ludwig van Beethovens (Schindler), 42 *n*, 133 *n*
Bizet, Georges (Alexandre-César-Léopold), 3 *n*
Boieldieu, François-Adrien, 34
Boito, Arrigo, vi
"Bombet," *see* Beyle
Borghi-Mamo, Adelaide, 128 and *n*
Borghi-Mamo, Erminia, 128 *n*
Bosio, Angiolina, 128 and *n*
Bülow, Hans von, viii, 13 and *n*, 14

Calzabigi, Raniero de', 39 *n*
Camilla, ossia Il Sotterraneo (Paër), 41 *n*
Carafa, Michele Enrico, Principe di Colobrano, 85 and *n*, 96 *n*
Carpani, Giuseppe, 40–41; quoted, 44–45, 52; 53, 134
Carvalho (Carvaille), Léon, 32 and *n*
Casti, Giovanni Battista, 39 *n*
castrati, 73–74, 109–10
Cenerentola (Rossini), 127
"Champfleury," *see* Husson
Champollion, Jean-François, 119 and *n*
Cherubini, Maria Luigi Carlo Zenobio Salvatore, 34, 96 *n*
Cheval de bronze, Le (Auber), 3 *n*, 77 *n*

Cimarosa, Domenico, 45, 118 *n*
Clapisson, Antoine-Louis, 3 and *n*
Comte Ory, Le (Rossini), 97 *n*, 98 *n*
Conservatoire Impérial de Musique (Paris), 77 *n*, 96 *n*, 116 *n*
Conservatoire Royal de Musique (Brussels), v
Covent Garden, Royal Opera House in (London), 37 *n*
Crémieux, Adolphe, 64–65

Danaïdes, Les (Salieri), 39 and *n*, 41
David, Félicien, 79–80
David(e), Giacomo, 104 and *n*
David(e), Giovanni, 39 *n*, 104 and *n*, 121
Désert, Le (David), 80 *n*
Diamants (Les) de la couronne (Auber), 3 *n*, 77 *n*
Don Carlos (Verdi), 129 *n*
Don Giovanni (Mozart), 28 and *n*
Don Pasquale (Donizetti), 128 *n*, 129 *n*
Donizetti, Domenico Gaetano Maria, 97 *n*, 104, 128 *n*
Doré, Gustave, vii *n*, 13 and *n*
Due Foscari, I (Verdi), 128 *n*
Duprez, Gilbert-Louis, 97–99

Epicurus, 83
"Erinnerungen an Rossini" (Wagner), vii, 9 and *n*
Euryanthe (Weber), 104 *n*

138

Index

Index

Index

Index

Salieri, Antonio, 39–41, 45, 134

Salle Ventadour (Paris), 1, 80 *n*

Schindler, Anton Felix, 42 *n*, 133 and *n*

Schopenhauer, Arthur, 83

Schöpfung, Die (Haydn), 48

Schumann, Robert Alexander, 135

Scudo, Pierre, 95 and *n*, 110, 127; quoted, 127–28

Séminaire Léon XIII (Louvain), x

Semiramide (Rossini), 85 *n*, 102–3, 127; "*Ah! quel giorno*," 102–3, 105

Serva padrona, La (Pergolesi), 46

Siège de Corinthe, Le (Rossini), 55 *n*, 97 *n*, 98 *n*

Siegfried (Wagner), 12 *n*, 26 *n*

Soirée (Une) chez Rossini à Beau-Séjour (Passy) 1858 (Michotte), vi, ix–x, 91 *n*

Sontag, Henriette, 104 and *n*, 120, 121, 128 *n*

Spontini, Gaspare Luigi Pacifico, 55

Stabat Mater, (Pergolesi), 46

Stabat Mater (Rossini), 16 *n*, 48 *n*, 94 *n*, 98 *n*, 128 *n*; *Quando Corpus morietur*, 48 and *n*; *Quis est homo*, 94 *n*

Stanislas II Augustus, King of Poland, 95 *n*

"Stendhal," *see* Beyle

Symphony No. 3 ("Eroica") (Beethoven), 39

Symphony No. 9 ("Choral") (Beethoven), 104 *n*

Tamberli(c)k, Enrico, 96 and *n*, 99

Tamburini, Antonio, 128 and *n*

Tancredi (Rossini), 45, 77 *n*; "*Di tanti palpiti*," 77 *n*

Tannhäuser (Wagner), ix, 1, 2 *n*, 3–4, 9, 12 and *n*, 14, 17, 19, 29, 30, 31–32, 55–56, 79, 86, 87, 132

Théâtre-Italien (Paris), 1, 32, 96 and *n*, 128

Thomas, Ambroise, 3 and *n*, 16, 129 *n*

Tristan und Isolde (Wagner), 2 and *n*, 14, 16 *n*, 26, 56

Troupenas, Eugène, 98 and *n*

Truinet, Charles-Louis-Étienne ("Charles Nuitter"), 12 *n*

Tschuddy, Louis-Théodore de, 39 *n*

Velluti, Giovanni Battista, 109 and *n*

Verdi, Fortunino Giuseppe Francesco, 91 *n*, 107–8, 128 *n*, 129 *n*

Viaggio a Reims, Il (Rossini), 104 *n*

Viardot-García, Pauline, 105 *n*

Vies de Haydn, Mozart et Métastase (Stendhal), 41 *n*

Villot, Frédéric, 13 and *n*

Visite (La) de R. Wagner à Rossini (Paris 1860) (Michotte), vi–ix, 4

Index

Wagner, Cosima (Liszt von Bülow), 13 *n*
Wagner, Minna (Planer), 12 and *n*
Wagner, Richard, vi, vii and *n*, and *passim*
Wagner family, 4
Wasielewski, Wilhelm Joseph von, 134 *n*
Weber, Carl Maria von, ix, 33–37, 50, 61, 75, 104 *n*

Wesendon(c)k, Mathilde, 2 *n*, 11

Zauberflöte, Die (Mozart), 48
Zelmira (Rossini), 33, 39, 52
Zucchini, Giovanni, 128 and *n*
Zukunftsmusik ("music of the future"), 17, 55, 69, 131–32